THE NEW
GARDENING
for
WILDLIFE

THE NEW
GARDENING
for
WILDLIFE

A GUIDE FOR NATURE LOVERS

BILL MERILEES

Whitecap Books
Vancouver / Toronto

The information in this book is true and complete to the best of our knowledge. The author and publisher disclaim any liability in connection with the use of this information. For additional information please contact Whitecap Books Ltd., 351 Lynn Avenue, North Vancouver, BC V7J 2C4.

Edited by Elaine Jones
Proofread by Kathy Evans
Interior design by Graham Sheard
Cover design by Roberta Batchelor
Photographs by Bill Merilees

Printed and bound in Canada

Canadian Cataloguing in Publication Data

Merilees, Bill
    The new gardening for wildlife

    Previous ed. has title: Attracting backyard wildlife.
    Includes bibliographical references and index.
    ISBN 1-55110-954-9

    1. Gardening to attract wildlife. I. Title. II. Title: Attracting backyard wildlife
QL59.M47 2000   635.9'6   C00-910069-5

The publisher acknowledges the support of the Canada Council for the Arts and the Cultural Services Branch of the Government of British Columbia in making this publication possible. We acknowledge the financial support of the Government of Canada through the Book Publishing Industry Development Program for our publishing activities.

To my father and mother, Welborne and Eva Merilees,
who, from my earliest recollections, initiated and kindled
an interest in doing things for backyard wildlife.
Many of their ideas grace these pages.

CONTENTS

ACKNOWLEDGEMENTS

This work began in earnest when the Federation of British Columbia Naturalists and the British Columbia Fish and Wildlife Branch of the Ministry of Environment Lands and Parks embarked upon the idea of fostering and promoting an interest in urban wildlife. *Gardening for Wildlife* has evolved far beyond the original goal, but the initial support of these groups is greatly appreciated.

Many individuals have provided assistance in many different ways. The following have been particularly helpful: Colin Bartlett, Don Blood, Gail Brown, Helen Butling, R. Wayne and Tessa Campbell, Dosie Crawford, Gerald and Ann Dennis, Bernie Gollop, Cris Guppy, Dave Kerridge, Ken and Marion Lambert, Donna McKean, Guy Monty, Alan Murray, Sylvia Pincott, Bernice Ross, David Stirling and Bruce Whitington.

Illustrative materials have been provided by Doug Kragh, Allyson MacBean and Chris Tunnock.

Special thanks are also due to R. Yorke Edwards for permission to quote his writings and to Liz Thunstrom of the Wildife Rescue Association of British Columbia for preparing the chapter about caring for sick and injured animals. Paul Steeves, a Wildlife Rescue Association Volunteer, kindly supplied the pictures used in this chapter.

The editorial advice of Elaine Jones who wrestled these ideas and materials into book form is very much appreciated.

Many thanks to my wife June and our family who helped, supported and tolerated my experiments into the fascinating field of wildlife gardening.

To all the above, a very special "Thank you."

CHAPTER 1
An Introduction to
Wildlife Gardening

Public surveys repeatedly indicate that North Americans commit large amounts of their leisure time and personal resources to the pursuit of wildlife appreciation. In Canada more than one-third of the population indicated in a national survey that they care for wildlife around their homes. In the United States, surveys of outdoor recreation activities list gardening and bird watching at or near the top. One of the primary purposes of this book is to bring these interests together.

The enjoyment of wildlife, like the enjoyment of art, music or literature, is a creative act. While it can be a matter of passive exposure, it may be enriched many times through active involvement. Through our windows, the world and its wildlife may be fascinating or dull, thrilling or frightening, ugly or beautiful according to our personal perspective. For people who wish to improve their gardens for wildlife, the quality of their experience will depend first on what they "sow" or develop and second on their ability to observe and interpret what they see.

In the past, truly great naturalists such as Charles Darwin, J. H. Fabre, and Gilbert White spent decades in their gardens observing, studying, experimenting and recording observations of plants and wild creatures. Gilbert White's classic *The Natural History and Antiquities of Selborne* (1788) had its genesis in a garden calendar begun in 1751. Reading this book and the classic works of Fabre and Darwin reveal simple pleasures any gardener might enjoy.

For Fabre, whose career had humble beginnings, there was one overriding desire. This is how he expressed it in his book, *The Wonders of Instinct*.

This was what I had wished for: a bit of land, oh not so very large, but fenced in to avoid the drawbacks of a public way; an abandoned, barren, sun scorched bit of land, favored by thistles and by wasps and bees. Yes, this was my wish, my dream always cherished, always vanishing into the mists of the future.

Perhaps no other private domain has been more appreciated or has produced more fascinating insights into the habits of insects. For Fabre, natural history was a passion; the writings that sprang from his indulgence are classic.

Few of us might wish for a garden favored by thistles, wasps and bees, although the joys we reap through careful observation could be equally satisfying. But for the backyard wildlife gardener, the diversity of plant and animal species we have to work with is both a joy and a headache! The joy comes from the variety of choice, the headache from having to make decisions.

Whatever our situation, local conditions such as climate, elevation, exposure and soil type will impose some limitations on our desires. Fortunately, most of the plants and animals we may wish to encourage have wide geographic ranges and broad levels of tolerance. Nonetheless, local knowledge will be very important.

Supplying all this information is beyond the scope of this book. However, rest assured that your community's nursery personnel, naturalists, nature centers, government agencies and other local experts will be able to provide much of the specific information you require. Do not hesitate to seek their advice or assistance. Since many heads are better than one, consulting these people may save you considerable effort, time and expense.

This book is written from a Pacific Northwest perspective, simply because this is my home environment. Of course native species of birds, insects and plants will vary from region to region, but the ideas and concepts put forward can be applied to all areas of North America. Whether in Florida or Alaska, all communities of animals and plants have the same needs: they must be able to feed, drink, find shelter and reproduce. The role of the wildlife gardener is to allow them to achieve their continued survival more easily.

Finally, there is much more to wildlife enjoyment than just looking for, and at, birds. This statement is not made to criticize birders or bird enthusiasts. It is made simply to remind us that there are tremendous rewards to be derived from non-avian life forms. While many of us think of birds first, let's not overlook other fascinating but perhaps more retiring wildlife.

Before we get into the how, what, when, where and why of backyard wildlife gardening, let's take a brief look at four important general considerations. These are: first, an understanding of the needs of all wildlife; second, knowing your personal preferences; third, recognizing your garden's unique features; and finally, setting realistic limits on your expectations. With these as your cornerstones, your chances of success will be greatly increased.

The Needs of All Wildlife

Simply stated, all wildlife has four basic requirements for survival. The first is sufficient space within which the remaining three—food, shelter and water—must occur.

The combination of these requirements to ensure survival varies greatly from one animal to another, even from one season to the next. No two animals, be they chipmunks, or squirrels or closely allied species of dragonflies, have identical needs.

Generally speaking, the larger and more diverse an area is in its terrain, variety of habitats and vegetation, the more types of wildlife and more individuals of each type it can accommodate.

When it comes to backyards of limited extent, most wildlife will be transient. Their presence will correspond only to the ability of the garden to meet their specific needs. For this reason most wildlife will move or shift (even migrate) from one area to another by day or season. A good example is the tree frog or spring peeper, which spends the spring breeding in ponds and the remainder of its active season in nearby foliage. Unless all the tree frog's needs are met in one area, the frog will move to another location. The challenge for the gardener who desires tree frogs year-round is to provide both an attractive pool and suitable surrounding vegetation.

When the general requirements of an animal are known, the wildlife gardener's challenge is to provide these in a smaller area than might be normal. This is the role of enhancement—the enriching of an area beyond its normal potential. Stocking a bird feeder is one of the simplest examples of enhancement.

Shelter	Shelter takes many forms, including protection from severe weather, availability of safe resting, roosting and hiding areas, and ample space to successfully rear young. In the normal backyard with limited space, all these cannot be provided, but through imaginative design and careful planning they can be improved considerably.
Food	Seasonal changes in natural food supply and individual preferences cause many kinds of wildlife to move from one area to another. These continual shifts in food availability and diet can be overcome in a number of ways. Means to this end include providing additional food supplies either by planting known and preferred food plants that provide a variety of seeds and fruits, developing feeding stations or attracting food sources, such as insects, into your area.
Water	The need for water is possibly the most overlooked and underestimated need of wildlife. Water is important for bathing and drinking. For many amphibians and insects it is essential for completing their life cycle. If you are fortunate enough to have a natural water source on your property, rejoice! If not, give serious consideration to developing one. Pools, baths and seeps all have their place as focal points in a backyard for urban wildlife.

Taking Stock

When planning your garden wildlife area, there are a number of important questions you ought to ask yourself before you begin.

1. What are your wildlife preferences?
   - butterflies?
   - frogs?
   - songbirds?
   - small mammals?
2. Before you buy a lot or property, consider the following questions:
   - How big an area will you have for the garden, front yard and backyard?
   - Does the property have a sunny or southerly exposure?

- Does the property have a good and varied selection of trees, shrubs and native plants?
- Does the property have a natural water supply (a spring, pond or small stream)? If so, will local regulations affect it?
- Does this property adjoin a park, woodcut, ravine or other wild area?
- Does the property have a varied and interesting topography?

3. Do any of your neighbors or potential neighbors share your interest in wildlife gardening? Might they wish to improve the wildlife potential of their gardens as well?
4. Are predators, particularly cats and dogs, going to be a continual nuisance?
5. Are young or noisy children going to present problems or a safety concern if you build a pool?
6. What local regulations are in place regarding property use, zoning, environmental regulations, noxious weeds and animals?
7. Is there a development plan for the neighborhood or community?
8. What kinds of soil are present and are they conducive to gardening?
9. Are there any tree diseases, insect pests or noxious weeds apparent?
10. Do the local authorities or neighbors regularly spray with herbicides or pesticides?

If your neighbors share your enthusiasm and interest, encourage their participation to considerably expand your effective wildlife area. Ask them. Nothing can be lost and there is much you could gain.

Unless an area has been bulldozed flat and scraped of all vegetation, every property should have some features that can be included in your wildlife landscape. Here are some features to cherish.

• dirt piles	• ditches	• rock piles
• boulders	• steep slopes	• logs
• stumps	• snags	• weed patches
• trees	• shrubs	

In fact, any landscape feature can be used to advantage. Trees, in particular deciduous trees and shrubs, should be protected from damage during construction. If these plants do not fit into your long-term plan, they can still prove to be very helpful while other more desirable plantings grow to a sufficient size and height for taking over.

Having considered the basic needs of wildlife, and having taken stock of what your property offers in the way of natural features, you should be able to determine what factor or factors are likely to limit wildlife use in your garden.

A limiting factor is a need that is not being met and so limits greater use by wildlife. By providing for this need, you stand to increase the use of your garden significantly. The one limiting factor that the gardener has little if any control over is climate. While it can be modified substantially over a small, limited area, such as by watering, the overall effect will generally be negligible.

Tailoring Your Expectations

Some time ago, a gentleman, quite knowledgeable about wildlife and natural history, told me that his winter works project had been the construction of a multi-apartment purple martin house for a children's home in our community. He had labored on this creation for many evenings over a number of months and was now about to erect his masterpiece. It was beautiful—but there are no purple martins in the area. His creation, although attractive, had very little practical value. Before he had even started this project, he should have asked himself, "What are the common bird species that regularly nest in this community?" and, "Which ones readily use nest boxes?"

Armed with this information and for the same effort at less cost, he could have built a dozen swallow boxes and robin nesting platforms. These would have had the potential of producing positive results.

Half the battle in encouraging and improving gardens for wildlife is knowing what to expect. Once this knowledge is at hand, matching animals—be they bugs, birds or bats—with their needs is much easier. In addition to knowing what animals are present, it is also important to know when they are present and what their habitat or food preferences might be. Since many migrate, and some hibernate or are very selective as to habitat, their appearance in any garden is often seasonal and brief. In my own garden the golden-crowned sparrow and Wilson's warbler visit for only a week or two each year. Any effort to entice them to stay longer is not likely to be successful.

Information on common animals in your area and when they are present can often be hard to find in your local library. Most books are too general in scope. Check first with your local museum. Perhaps they have a natural history section. A naturalist club, Audubon Society chapter or nature center should be able to direct you to someone who can help with information specific to your community. Your local tourist information bureau or community recreation commission will often have contacts for these groups. Government agencies responsible for environmental concerns, particularly fish and wildlife or park naturalist interpretation programs, might also be able to help.

Having a garden dedicated to wildlife has both positive and negative sides. Wildlife can be enjoyable to observe, but if they get into the walls, attic or some other part of your house, they can do serious damage. Before launching on a wildlife garden program homeowners must be aware of the potential problems and take the steps required so they can enjoy their garden visitors and at the same time feel comfortable with their presence.

The following chapters will list some of the common species you might find in your area and give you some suggestions for encouraging their presence, as well as general information.

CHAPTER 2
Gardening for Butterflies

For color and variety in a garden setting, butterflies are perhaps second only to birds. In many ways, observing butterflies is easier than watching birds. While birds flit from branch to branch and are often obscured by foliage, butterflies remain out in the open in full view. Butterflies, however, are summer visitors only over most northern areas, and their dependence on ambient temperatures restricts their activity periods to the warmer portion of the day. For butterflies to take flight, air temperatures generally must be above 60°F (16°C).

From monarchs to skippers, North American butterfly species number in the hundreds. Virtually every area populated by humans has a variety of species, although warmer areas of the south have significantly higher numbers and variety of species than more northern locations. In the south, they are also in flight all twelve months of the year.

The practice of importing exotic vegetation for much of the landscaping in urban areas does not encourage native butterfly populations. Most imported vegetation does not produce the appropriate kinds of flowers or have the properties required for butterflies to complete their life cycles. Therefore it is quite amazing that a few butterflies have overcome this difficulty and may be seen in the hearts of our largest cities. In our suburbs quite a number of species remain reasonably common and well known—thanks, in part, to private gardens. Some of the larger and more colorful moths can be seen here too.

The needs of butterflies are quite simple. The first is a warm, sunny location protected from strong prevailing winds, with ample sites for perching, resting and sunning.

The second requirement is a profusion, both in number and variety, of sweet-scented, colorful flowers. Select flowers to ensure a progression of flowering from early spring until late autumn. In the south, where butterflies remain active all year round, select winter-flowering species as well. Some flowering plants are more favored by butterflies than others. Many species, particularly moths, have a specialized anatomy that is flower-specific when it comes to being able to feed. Wise butterfly gardeners keep their eyes open and allow the butterflies themselves to dictate the plants the gardeners bring into their gardens. Be aware that many popular cultivated flowers have lost their fragrance during horticultural development.

In addition to nectar-producing flowers, the adult females of butterflies and some moth species also require specific plants on which to lay their eggs. The affinity of monarchs for milkweeds and spicebush swallowtails for the spicebush are well documented. Most other butterflies have similar preferences. Without their host plants, which will nourish the larvae and allow the caterpillars to grow through to pupation, these butterflies would not be able to complete their life cycle. Butterfly gardeners need to be aware of these very specific needs if they wish to enjoy a broad range of butterflies.

During hot weather, water—not nectar— is a butterfly's more important need. While most butterflies will obtain the water they require from the flowers they visit, many species seem to enjoy a damp open area from which to drink. Butterflies are often seen congregating along streams, on wet rocks and even damp pavement. In a wildlife garden, water can be provided as a "seep." A seep is simply an area that is kept moist by a small but constant supply of water. A shallow pool edge with coarse sand or the overflow from a birdbath or air conditioner are three possible water sources.

Puddling

Around good drinking sources, such as damp ditches, lake shores and pool edges, butterflies often gather for "puddle parties." Puddling, as this is known, can attract large numbers of individuals to a small area. Naturally saline soils are favored. Adding a little table salt to backyard seeps has been suggested to improve their performance. Swallowtails in particular are prone to puddling.

One of the most important requirements of a butterfly garden is that it be a pesticide-free zone. Herbicides and pesticides may relieve an immediate problem, but more often than not the damage reaches a lot further than the original target. This extends to biological controls as well, and the aerial spraying of Btk is becoming a classic example.

Across North America the forest industry regards the possible spread of the gypsy moth with great concern. To combat this potentially serious pest, a number of areas have been broadcast-sprayed with the bacterial insecticide Btk (*Bacillus thuringiensis kurstaki*). This control is especially toxic to butterfly and moth larvae and poses a serious threat to all butterfly populations whose caterpillars are active at the time of spraying. Even more worrisome is the genetic engineering of agricultural crop species. Wind-blown corn pollen, engineered to include Btk, for example, has been shown to be toxic to monarch butterfly larvae feeding on nearby milkweed plants.

Oregano

Common oregano or wild marjoram (*Origanum vulgare*) attracts a diverse assemblage of butterflies to my garden. It produces clusters of mauve blooms on stems 12 to 18 inches (30 to 45 cm) high, tolerates neglect and does well in dry, well-drained soil. In early July, about the time the local skippers and hairstreaks appear, the oregano blooms, providing these butterflies with a favored nectar source. A variety of leaf-cutting bees and syrphid and tachinid flies are also attracted to this perennial, pleasantly scented herb.

Swallowtails

These are our showiest butterflies. They are large, colorful, common and active, flying from late spring until early autumn. All are black or have strong black markings: many are strikingly patterned with yellow. Most, but not all, have elongated projections on their hind wings resembling swallow tails. There are about 25 North American species.

Plants such as *Buddleia*, *Ceanothus* and *Centranthus* should do well in most gardens and bear small tubular flowers ideal for producing nectar. Swallowtail larvae, or caterpillars, are large and brightly patterned with yellow, orange, green and black. When disturbed they have the ability to evert their osmeterium (a soft horn-like projection from the head) that gives off a foul odor.

Butterfly	Larval Food Plants
Tiger swallowtail (*Papilio* species)	Cottonwood (*Populus* species)
	Wild cherry (*Prunus* species)
	Willow (*Salix* species)
	Maple (*Acer* species)
	Alder (*Alnus* species)
Anise swallowtail (*Papilio zelicaon*)	Fennel (*Foeniculum vulgare*)
	Dill (*Anethum graveolens*)
Swallowtails (other species) (*Papilio* species)	Cow parsnip (*Heracleum* species)
	Spring gold and biscuitroot (*Lomatium* species)
	Spicebush (*Calycanthus* species)

Cabbage White

This European import is perhaps the most common and well-known butterfly in North America. It has a number of native cousins that are simply called "whites."

While most whites lay their eggs on species in the mustard family (Cruciferae), especially cabbage, some lay their eggs on coniferous trees, such as pines and hemlocks.

Butterfly	Larval Food Plants
Cabbage white (*Pieris rapae*)	Cabbage *(Brassica oleracea)*
	Mustards (Cruciferae family)
	Nasturtium *(Tropaeolum majus)*
Native whites (*Pieris* and *Pontia* species)	Mustards (Cruciferae family; *Draba, Thlaspi, Lepidium* and *Sisymbrium)*
(*Neophasia* species)	Douglas-fir (*Pseudotsuga menziesii)*
	Hemlocks *(Tsuga* species)
	Pines *(Pinus* species)

Sulfurs

These are the yellow to orange (sulfur-colored) grassland and farm-land butterflies usually associated with open grasslands. Many have black wingtips or other dark markings.

Butterfly	Larval Food Plants
Sulfurs	Sweet-clover (*Melilotus* species)
(*Colias* species)	Clovers (*Trifolium* species)

Blues, Coppers and Hairstreaks

This group of smallish butterflies has many members. The blues and coppers are indeed blue or copper in color, while the hairstreaks have derived their name from the fine, filamentous projections from the hind wings—a diminutive swallow tail–like structure.

These are common butterflies, and the food plants of their caterpillars are numerous and varied. Many gardens have quite a variety.

Butterfly	Larval Food Plants
Blues	Spireas (*Spiraea* species)
(*Celastrina* species)	Dogwoods (*Cornus* species)
(*Icarica* species)	Violets (*Viola* species)
(*Lycaeides* species)	Lupines (*Lupinus* species)
Coppers	Dock (*Rumex* species)
(*Lycaena* species)	
Hairstreaks	Clovers (*Trifolium* species)
(*Satyrium* species)	Sweet-clovers (*Melilotus* species)

Brush-Footed Butterflies

Included among this large family are the painted ladies, mourning cloaks, red admiral, tortoiseshells and anglewings. All are characterized by their front legs, which are greatly reduced in size with numerous hair-like scales—hence the name brush-footed. When examined closely they appear to have only four legs. Many of these species migrate north as summer progresses. Gardens with a good patch of stinging nettle will attract many of these species.

Mourning cloaks are one of our larger, more common butterflies and one of the earliest to appear each spring in northern areas. Because it is the adults that overwinter, this is our longest-lived butterfly, up to 10 months. The bristly caterpillars are gregarious, clustering together on willows and elms.

Butterfly	Larval Food Plants
Mourning cloaks	Elms (*Uemus* species)
(*Nymphalis antiopa*)	Willows (*Salix* species)
Painted ladies	Thistles (*Cirsium* species)
(*Vanessa* species)	Mallows (Malvaceae family)
	Pearly everlasting (*Anaphalis margaritacea*)
	Stinging nettle (*Urtica dioica*)
Red admiral	Stinging nettle (*Urtica dioica*)
(*Vanessa atalanta*)	
Tortoiseshells	Stinging nettle (*Urtica dioica*)
(*Aglais* and *Roddia* species)	
Anglewings	Stinging nettle (*Urtica dioica*)
(*Polygonia* species)	

Admirals

Not related to the red admiral, above, these admirals are also active, colorful butterflies that are somewhat territorial. They often survey their territory from a convenient prominent perch and then fly out after other butterflies that would trespass. Often they are attracted to baits, and have been observed feeding on rotting fruit, even animal carcasses and feces. They can become a common garden butterfly.

Butterfly	Larval Food Plants
Lorquin's admiral (western)	Willow (*Salix* species)
(*Limenitis lorquini*)	Cottonwood (*Populus* species)
White admiral (eastern)	Cherry (*Prunus* species)
(*Limenitis arthemis*)	Apple (*Malus* species)
	Spirea (*Spiraea* species)

Antennae of Butterflies, Skippers and Moths

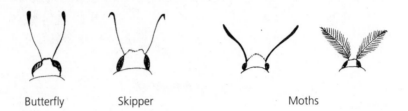

Butterfly   Skipper   Moths

Skippers

This distinct group of butterflies is easily identified by the hooked tips of their antennae. (See illustration, above.) When at rest, their front and hind wings are held at different angles, somewhat resembling the conformation of a fighter-bomber. Most of the more common species are mustard brown in color.

Their caterpillars are seldom seen, because they often roll a leaf of their host plant around themselves. Larval food plants are grasses (Gramineae family).

Monarchs and Viceroys

Monarchs are more common east of the Rocky Mountains but occasionally numbers spill over to the west coast. Caterpillars of this species are wonderful—striped with yellow, black and white. These large, orange and black butterflies are noted migrants (see Butterfly Migration, page 17) and at their winter roosts in Mexico and southern California they congregate in the thousands. The viceroy is a monarch look-alike (see Butterfly Mimicry, page 19).

Butterfly	Larval Food Plants
Monarch	Milkweed (*Asclepias* species)
(*Danaus plexippus*)	Dogbane (*Apocynum* species)
Viceroy	Willow (*Salix* species)
(*Limenitis archippus*)	Poplar (*Populus* species)
	Trembling aspen (*Populus tremuloides*)

Large Moths

Luna, cecropia and polyphemus moths are members of the silk-worm moth family whose larvae, or caterpillars, pupate in silken cocoons. These are large moths, some with a wingspan of 6 inches (15 cm). Many are brightly colored. The males have large feathery antennae used to detect the scent trails of the female. The adults do not feed. After mating, the female lays her eggs on an appropriate host plant, then dies.

These large, handsome moths are most often found in the morning, clinging to walls and screens, around porch lights that have been left on overnight.

The large caterpillars are seldom seen, as they frequent the foliage of fairly large trees. The larvae are often green and have spines, some of which may inflict a sting similar to that of stinging nettles.

Butterfly	Larval Food Plants
Cecropia	Cherry (*Prunus* species)
(*Hyalophora cecropia*)	Maple (*Acer* species)
	Willow (*Salix* species)
Luna	Persimmon (*Diospyros* species)
(*Actias luna*)	Walnut (*Juglans* species)
	Hickory (*Carya* species)
	Sweet gum (*Liquidambar* species)
Polyphemus	Oak (*Quercus* species)
(*Antheraea*	Maple (*Acer* species)
polyphemus)	Birch (*Betula* species)
	Elm (*Ulmus* species)
Sphinx	Tomato (*Lycopersicon* species)
(Family Sphingidae,	Potato (*Solanum* species)
many species)	Tobacco (*Nicotiana* species)

Some Good Nectar-Producing Plants Attractive to Butterflies

Native Plants
- Stonecrop (*Sedum* species)
- Cow parsnip (*Heracleum* species)
- Milkweed (*Asclepias* species)
- Wild lilac (*Ceanothus* species)
- Pearly everlasting (*Anaphalis margaritacea*)
- Yarrow (*Achillea millefolium*)
- Asters (Michaelmas daisy) (*Aster* species)
- Thistle (*Cirsium* species)
- Goldenrod (*Solidago* species)

Introduced Plants
- Butterfly bush (*Buddleia davidii*)
- Lantana (*Lantana* species)
- Lavender (*Lavandula* species)
- Lilac (*Syringa* species)
- Oregano (*Origanum* species)
- Sweet william (*Dianthus* species)
- Daisies/Chrysanthemums (*Chrysanthemum* species)
- Gloriosa daisy (*Rudbeckia hirta*)
- Cornflower/Bachelor buttons (*Centaurea* species)

Introduced Weeds
- Burdock (*Arctium* species)
- Thistle (*Cirsium* and *Carduus* species)
- Sow thistle (*Sonchus* species)
- Dandelion (*Taraxacum officinale*)
- Hairy cat's-ear (*Hypochaeris radicata*)

What Are Weeds?

A popular definition of a weed is: a plant growing in the wrong place. This term is also often applied to plants that have become naturalized as a result of an accidental introduction. Many weeds are quite attractive and colorful. Others provide considerable value to wildlife. Still others have become invasive, noxious pests that are a serious nuisance that threaten native habitats and agricultural production.

Butterfly Migration

The celebrated migration of the monarch butterfly from its northern range to its roosting sites in Mexico and California is one of the wonders of the insect world. It takes two, possibly three different generations of monarchs to complete this journey. From north to south, it could span 27 degrees of latitude (nearly 1,900 miles/3000 km) from the Canadian prairies to Northern Mexico!

Other species, such as the tortoiseshells and painted ladies, have been observed moving southward in numbers, but whether this is a migration or just a local movement is unclear.

On the monarch's northward journey the presence of milkweed (*Asclepias* species) allows them to deposit their eggs, initiating the next generation that will carry on the journey. On their southern route, bright, showy, nectar-producing flowers, such as daisies and goldenrods, sustain their progress. As the autumn proceeds, gardens with copious numbers of bright butterfly flowers become resting and feeding stations. A garden full of monarchs must be a wonderful sight!

4JCs–The Butterfly Counts

Butterfly enthusiasts have initiated butterfly counts, patterned after the Audubon Society's CBCs (Christmas Bird Counts). The butterfly counts provide an inventory of numbers and species seen flying on a particular day. These Fourth of July Counts (hence 4JC) can take place

Woolly Bear Caterpillar

The large family of tiger moths (Arctiidae family) has many common species. These moths are not often seen due to their nocturnal activity period, but just about every gardener is familiar with their caterpillars, the woolly bears. Most feed on grasses around the periphery of our gardens and are not a serious concern. Larvae are generally very hairy, almost bristly in appearance, and are commonly rusty orange and black.

any time butterflies are active. They are coordinated by the North American Butterfly Association.

Just as many bird enthusiasts keep lists of the birds that visit their gardens, butterfly gardeners who record the appearance and habits of each species will find it adds to the enjoyment of gardening.

Butterfly Attractants and Pheromones

Hiking along a creekbed in Olympic National Park in Washington State, I came across a pair of discarded hiking boots. They were covered with at least three species of butterflies (see photo), almost all males.

Butterfly or Moth Bait

Mix these following ingredients and let stand for 12 to 24 hours
- 1 quart (1 L) low-alcohol beer
- ½ pound (450 g) brown sugar
- 1 tablespoon (15 mL) rum
- 1 slice brown bread
- 1 apple, cut into small pieces

To set out the bait, cut pieces of 2-inch (5-cm) thick sponge into 3 x 3-inch (7.5 x 7.5-cm) squares. Soak these in the solution and tie them or place them on trees, posts etc.

In the animal world many species release odors known as pheromones, perfumes used to bring the genders together for mating. If you examine the antennae of some of the larger moths, you will notice the male antennae are much larger than those of the females. The antennae are scent-catching devices, and since the males seek out the females, their antennae are larger.

In the case of the "butterfly boots" the leather, probably infused with human sweat, was producing an appropriate perfume to distract these species from their real quest. It has also been suggested that since some butterflies are attracted to carrion, feces, and even dead snakes, this might be a clue as to why the boots had been discarded!

Butterflies have also been observed to be attracted to automobile tail and signal lights. One of my backyard experiments will be a mobile constructed of shards of red, amber and white glass to test this possibility as a butterfly lure.

Butterfly Hibernation—Surviving Over Winter

In northern regions butterflies use varied strategies to survive winter. Some hibernate, overwintering as adults (mourning cloak, commas and anglewings), some as pupae (many swallowtails and skippers), some as larvae (Lorquin's admiral) and some in the egg stage (some hairstreaks). Some utilize a number of these. Some, like the monarch, migrate to warmer environments.

Butterflies that overwinter as adults seek out hollow trees, sheds, wood piles and log piles for hibernation sites. Some of these can be incorporated around the fringes or in a quiet corner of a garden. Some success has been achieved with hibernation houses, a bird house design with two vertical slits ⅜ inch (.95 cm) and 5 to 8 inches (12.5 to 20 cm) long rather than the usual circular hole. A lining of cedar bark to round out the inside will make these spaces more natural.

Hummingbird Moths

As dusk falls a number of large moths begin to move around night-flowering plants such as evening primrose. The large sphinx or hawk moths resemble hummingbirds in size, shape and manner of flight and are often called hummingbird moths. Their large, long, hairless larvae are known as hornworms for the soft spine-like process near the caterpillar's rear end. As a group, the sphinx moths contain some interesting species. Some day-flying species that often visit lilac flowers have large clear patches in their wings and strongly resemble bumblebees.

Butterfly Mimicry

In the struggle to live long enough to procreate, many animals have developed strategies to extend their life expectancy. Among butterflies, one of the best-known of these is mimicry. A good example is monarchs and viceroys. The monarch is large, slow-flying and vividly colored. It makes virtually no effort to conceal its presence from would-be predators. Why? In its larval development it feeds on milkweed species, most of which pass on a number of their toxins to the caterpillar. This makes the adult monarch quite unpalatable and would-be predators quickly learn to avoid monarchs.

In another butterfly family altogether, the viceroy is a monarch look-alike. Viceroy caterpillars feed on willows, poplars and aspen. The viceroy is edible, but it deceives those predators that have learned to avoid the monarch.

Anise swallowtail chrysalis
on thin cedar stake

Chrysalis Perches

Towards the very end of the caterpillar stage in a butterfly's life cycle, the larva becomes very active. Up to this point it has remained quite sedentary, gorging on plant food. The purpose of this sudden activity is to distribute caterpillars over a wider area so that they do not pupate in close proximity to one another.

For many species, the pupal stage guarantees survival of the species over the winter season. Gardening practices that remove dead branches, flower stalks and debris also risk removing many of the chrysalises. I have used thin red-cedar stakes, not more than ¼ inch (.6 cm) in diameter and circles of lathing screen as chrysalis perches for anise swallowtails in my garden.

Life Cycle of the Anise Swallowtail

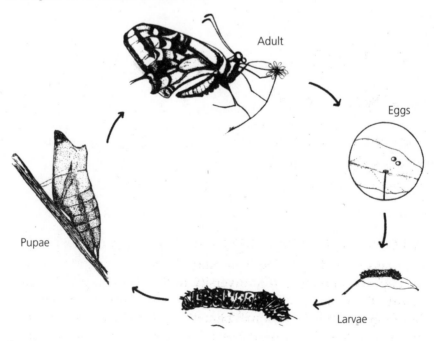

Adult

Eggs

Larvae

Pupae

CHAPTER 3
Insect-Friendly Gardens

Of all backyard wildlife, insects and spiders are the least under-
stood, the most neglected and overlooked, and yet they are among
the most fascinating. To appreciate these wild creatures and to
observe their intricate habits requires patience, skill and a little
luck. J. H. Fabre, the French natural scientist who devoted his life
to unraveling the mysteries of these six- and eight-legged arthro-
pods, was exceptional both as an observer and as a writer.

Insects bring joy to us in many ways. For some it is through their
music. Many species have their personal repertoire of song. For
each, the sound is both limited and species-specific. On warm, still
summer evenings these choruses may combine into a symphony of
sound. On summer afternoons the loud *snap-crack-snap* of long-
horned grasshoppers announces warm dry conditions. The fuzzy
buzz of cicadas is another familiar sound that has intrigued people
with its ventriloquistic qualities.

For delicate beauty and precision of form, what about a fresh
cobweb of an orb spider? When doused with dew, each tiny
droplet splits light into a rainbow of color. Our visual sense is further stimulated by the metallic sparkle of the buprestid beetles, or
the brilliance of a butterfly's wing, where each minute scale adds its
pixel of color. Examples are endless.

Insects and spiders are primarily warm-season wildlife. Of the
thousands present (more than 90,000 have been described for North
America), we can discuss only a handful of the common groups.
These, of necessity, must be the large, showy, easily identified and
common ones present in most gardens. The right conditions will
bring many of these, wanted or unwanted, into the average garden.

No plant is totally immune to the ravages of insects and no garden can be made insect free—nor should it be. As well as being

important pollinators of plants, insects and spiders are the prime food of other insects, reptiles, amphibians, birds and small mammals. Because of insects' importance in the food chain, having a really bug-infested yard can have its advantages! For those gardeners who wish to appreciate wildlife in its broadest sense, spiders and insects offer a challenge not easily dismissed.

A lesson that organic gardeners understand well is that many interesting insects help control some of the noxious pest species. Perhaps the best example is the ladybird beetle, which, as both larva and adult, feeds on aphids. Some gardeners actually purchase these predators for this purpose.

Cricket Boards

Safe places in which crickets can hide and sing are one feature that is easily added to any garden. A scrap piece of wood or a flat rock that rests loosely about ½ inch (1.5 cm) above the ground are ideal places for male crickets to establish singing stations. To separate male from female crickets see illustration below.

As we wander our gardens and begin observing the myriad of life forms present (there are probably more than a thousand kinds of insect in your garden alone!), we soon begin to notice differences from one individual to another. Sight is the faculty, seeing is an art, and like any art, it can be improved with practice. Observing insects and spiders can be incredibly rewarding and appeals to the child in all of us. To appreciate, understand and accept their place in our living space is a challenge to last a lifetime.

Field Crickets

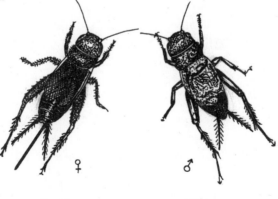

Female   Male

Gardens with a somewhat untidy appearance have a great many insect niches. Most insects will be present in our gardens at all times but will be seen only from time to time. As opportunity permits, as the gardener comes across new forms, a field guide to the various insect groups will help put names to this menagerie. The study of insects offers quite a challenge. Each group often has thousands of members.

From sowbugs to praying mantis to crab spiders the diversity in form of the arthropod assemblage is a study unto itself. Not knowing who this cast of characters is, or the relationships among the various groups, frustrates even the scientist. Even with specimens in hand, a specialist for one small group—bees for instance—will often be hard-pressed to give you their name, scientific or common!

When someone asked the eminent scientist J. B. S. Haldane what he could tell about the Creator from what he saw around him, his reply was, "The Lord had an inordinate fondness for beetles!" Beetles are estimated to account for about one-half of all the life forms on earth.

The following is a partial list of some of the more common insects and spiders found in our gardens. Remember that all spiders are venomous and many bees can sting. Although their bites and stings are generally not harmful, one should always be careful when handling or working around them.

Some Common Backyard Insects, Spiders and Their Relatives

Sowbugs and Pillbugs

These first cousins are terrestrial relatives of a primarily marine group of organisms known as isopods. They are commonly found under loose bark and downed wood. Rather than six legs, like insects, they have seven pairs of leg-like appendages. Sowbugs are dull gray in color. Pillbugs are bright black and shiny. When disturbed, pillbugs roll up into a pea-sized "pill," hence their name. On a smooth down-hill slope, like a driveway, they can roll for great distances!

Millipedes and Centipedes

These are another pair of "cousins" that share a long segmented body form. Usually dull-colored and slow moving, millipedes derive their name from many legs, four on each body segment. *Milli*, meaning thousand, and *ped*, meaning leg, gives them their common name. Some have bright yellow spots.

Unlike the vegetarian millipedes, centipedes are active, fast-moving predators that can inflict a bite. They are often rusty brown in color. Two long legs per segment give the appearance of 100, hence the prefix *centi*.

Spiders

Daddy-longlegs, or **Harvestmen:** These spider relatives are common and well known to most gardeners; their small, oval body and extremely long, slender legs are easily recognized.

Orb Spiders: The large, beautiful spider webs that we see in late summer and early autumn are the creations of these large, round-bodied spiders. Other spiders create different types of webs, such as dome weavers, which produce finer, more elaborate structures.

Crab Spiders: Flowers are where this spider waits in ambush to grasp its prey. The arrangement of the larger front legs has evolved for this grasping purpose.

Grasshoppers

These long-legged jumpers, well known to most of us, come in a variety of colors. Some are brightly colored and some show bright flashes of red or yellow during their noisy, snapping flight.

Katydids are the large greenish grasshoppers found primarily in eastern North America. The males are known for their singing abilities.

Insect Choruses

The accomplished sound producers in the insect symphony are grasshoppers, crickets and cicadas. The purpose of their singing is for males to advertise their presence to females. The sound is created by rubbing one body part, usually a leg or wing, over another.

The volume of sound increases through spring, reaching a peak in late summer. Most gardens will have suitable habitats for a number of these singing species to be enjoyed. However it is in the tropics that these singers really come into their own.

Field Crickets

These are the common and widely distributed shiny black crickets of gardens, fields and roadsides. Like katydids, they are noted songsters.

Cicadas

The pulsating buzz of the male cicada makes this insect more often heard than seen. They tend to live and sing from trees. Often it is the shed case, or exoskeleton, of the nymph that indicates the presence of adult cicadas. A number of cicada species have a long life cycle and are known by the number of years it takes them to pass from egg to adult, e.g., 13 year or 17 year, etc.

Praying Mantis

The distinctive appearance of the praying mantis is more often seen in pictures than in life. They are voracious predators—a treat to have, and to watch, in any garden. Their beady eyes, genuflect forearms and form are known primarily to southern gardeners. Two introduced mantises are found more widely.

Mantises lay eggs in nests resembling a small wasp's nest. For gardeners who would like to see mantises in their garden, many biological supply houses sell the egg cases for this and educational purposes.

Beetles

Ground Beetles: One of our more common beetles, they generally hide by day and are active by night. Ground beetles move quickly when uncovered.

Ladybird Beetles: Ladybirds are predacious beetles in both their larval and adult forms and hence are very beneficial in our gardens. Their main foods are aphids and scale insects. Though universally present in small numbers, the adults sometimes overwinter in large groups of many thousands.

Scarab Beetles: These large and often colorful beetles are more often harmful than helpful. They include the dung beetles, June beetles, leaf chaffers and rhinoceros beetles.

Long-horned Beetles: This is another diverse group noted for their long antennae. Many are large, colorful and attractive. Most emerge from dead or dying wood.

Ladybird Beetle Life Cycle

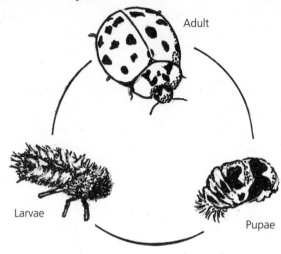

Syrphid Flies or Hover Flies

If you mistake these flies for bees you could be excused. In color, size, appearance and in many of their habits they mimic wasps and bees. There are many common species. Many like to hover (hence the name) and often they frequent flowers. Some even have the ability to buzz! While their appearance and behavior strongly suggest bees, syrphid flies do not sting.

Ants

Ants are colonial, social insects found almost everywhere. It is the exceptional garden that does not have an ant colony somewhere, usually in the ground. Although some may bite, they are generally harmless. A few build extensive dome-shaped nests 40 inches (1 m) or more high. A number of species tend aphids, milking them for their honeydew.

Bees and Wasps

Mud-daubing Wasps: These large, thread-waisted wasps are very partial to damp locations where mud is available. They build nests of mud in cracks or crevices, where they feed spiders, grasshoppers and caterpillars to their larvae.

Leafcutting Bees: Most often it is the "fancy work" of these bees that is noticed, rather than the bee itself. They usually make their nests in the ground or a natural cavity. Mason bees, also known as orchard bees, are part of the leafcutting bee family. They are important fruit tree pollinators (see sidebar).

Bumblebees: Large, often yellow and black, fuzzy bees are common virtually everywhere. They are colonizers and often take over an abandoned mouse nest, which becomes their hive.

Honey Bees: There is only one honey bee, and it is common everywhere in North America. Most live in manufactured hives but wild swarms will use tree cavities.

Yellow-jackets and Hornets: These are the "nasties" of our garden environments, often feared by humans because of their stinging abilities. They build large paper nests where they feed their young chewed-up parts of other insects.

The Orchard or Mason Bee

Sometimes called the blue orchard bee on account of its dark metallic blue color, this benign solitary bee is about two-thirds the size of the average honey bee— about ½ inch (1 cm) long. As a pollinator it is incredibly efficient, up to 95%. Honey bees are reported to achieve only a 5% efficiency, and they are on the decline, making mason bees even more valuable to fruit and vegetable growers.

The female mason bee is very particular when choosing a nesting site. Because she

Social Insects

Many species of bees and ants have developed elaborate societies based on a caste system that includes queens, workers and drones. Many, like the paper wasps and mound-building ants, build elaborate nests, some of enormous size. One colony of ants in Oregon is reported to have built a nest, over a number of years, that contained enough material to make a full load for one large dump truck—more than 8 cubic yards!

The best known and most economically important social insect is the honey bee. Honey bee workers have a language that communicates to other workers, by the odor they carry back to the hive, the type and location of good nectar-producing flowers.

In our gardens there are a great many species of these social insects (about 17,000 known in North America). Honey bees, bumblebees and mason wasps are three types that can be induced to use artificial nesting structures.

cannot excavate, she searches out a naturally occurring tubular hole or cavity. With
much of the native vegetation removed
from urban areas, this is not always an easy
task.

The French entomologist Fabre invented
an artificial method to induce nesting so
he could study the species of mason bees
that visited his garden. This was the pro-
totype for methods now being used in
North America (see photo), where blocks
of wood are drilled with $5/16$-inch (8-mm)
holes and placed in gardens and orchards.

Holes in a post for mason
bee use

The female mason bee does all the work of collecting the pollen,
mixing it with nectar and placing it in the cavity selected. On this
she lays a rather large, for her size, $1/8$-inch (3 to 3.5 mm) egg and
then seals off the chamber with a wall of mud—hence the name
"mason" bee. The process continues until the tubular hole is filled.

Female eggs are laid deepest in the hole, males towards the
entrance. The males hatch first, at about the time the first flowering fruit trees burst into bloom, and they emerge to wait for the
females. Mating then takes place and the cycle repeats.

Some Plants Attractive to Common Colorful Insects

Just about every plant growing in or near your garden will have its
attendant insects. A few of these will be beneficial, some will be
harmful or a nuisance, but most will be benign. It is a mighty sterile garden that does not have a rich diversity of insect forms. When
it comes to bees, especially honey bees, your local apiarists will tell
you what types of flowers are good honey and pollen producers for
your area. The following chart lists a few species of plants. Your
local nursery should be able to give you more ideas.

Trees and Shrubs	Season	Comments
Willows (*Salix* species)	Early spring	Pussywillows and foliage attract bees, beetles and flies.
Spireas (*Spiraea* species)	Late spring to early summer	Attractive to beetles.
Heaths and heathers (*Erica* species)	Early spring	Attractive to bees.
Cotoneaster (*Cotoneaster* species)	Late spring	Flowers in spring; fruit in autumn and winter attracts birds.

Flowers	Season	Comments
Cow parsnip (*Heracleum* species)	Late spring	Flowers attractive to bees, flies and beetles, etc.
Red clover (*Trifolium pratense*)	Late spring	A bumblebee favorite.
Tower of jewels (*Echium wildpretii*)	Summer	Colorful interesting flowers favored by bees.
Viper's bugloss (*Echium vulgare*)	Summer	As above.
Fennel (*Foeniculum vulgare*)	Summer	Attractive to a nice variety of bees.
Oregano (*Origanum vulgare*)	Summer	Addictive to a variety of bees, flies and small butterflies.
Policeman's helmet (*Impatiens glandulifera*)	Summer	An annual that likes moist soil. The large pink flowers attract bees.
Asters and Michaelmas daisy (*Aster* species)	Summer and autumn	A good general source of nectar and pollen.
Dandelion (*Taraxacum* species)	Early spring	Many insects, especially honey bees, find dandelions a good early pollen source.
Pearly everlasting (*Anaphalis margaritacea*)	Summer	Good for many species, including some of the smaller butterflies.
Goldenrods (*Solidago* species)	Late summer and autumn	The bright, mustard-yellow flower heads attract some interesting bugs.
Thistles (*Cirsium* species)	Summer and autumn	Bumblebees and butterflies enjoy this nectar source.

CHAPTER 4

Water Gardening for Aquatic Species

One of the most soothing and relaxing features of a garden is a well-located and nicely landscaped pool. A trickle of running water adds even more to the ambience. Just about every species that visits your garden will benefit in some way from a pool. Specialized nurseries carry everything you need to build and stock a pool, from pumps to fish. (In this book *pond* refers to a naturally fed or occurring body of water and *pool* refers to a manufactured one.) One thing the water garden specialists do not sell are the lovely diversity of interesting insects—among them damselflies and dragonflies, mayflies and caddisflies, water beetles and water striders—that find their way into every pool, completely unaided. (Amphibians and reptiles with similar aquatic affinities will also be attracted to a pond. These are discussed in Chapters 5 and 6.)

Other interesting pond life includes mollusks (clams and snails) and crustaceans, such as fairy shrimp and crayfish. Some of these will need assistance in getting overland to your pool. Often they come attached to vegetation when it is being transplanted.

A garden pool, in addition to being soothing or pretty, can add a focal point to your garden, provide a drinking or bathing location for local wildlife, and allow some species of aquatic or partially terrestrial animals to breed and/or complete their life cycles. A water source is probably the single most important element for encouraging diversity in your wildlife garden.

In my own garden I have four pools, each with a different purpose and focus. One is for salamanders, one for frogs, one has crayfish and the last is open to everything, including goldfish. Insects have the choice of using them all and according to their selection run a variety of risks depending on the tastes of the other residents.

Most pools, once carefully planted and then left alone, will develop their own balance and do very nicely unattended. Be patient when the plantings are becoming established. Overfeeding fish or over-fertilizing plants can quickly undo a pool's natural balance. The array and option of treatments available for pools is bewildering, yet in 15 years I have never had to be concerned with pH, water clarity, water quality or disease in any of my pools. Other than topping up the water level now and then and removing dead, excessive or unwanted vegetation, these pools have found a natural harmony with minimal maintenance.

Think carefully about including fish—primarily goldfish or koi—in your pool. These fish clean up on everything edible, both plant and animal. They are graceful and beautiful, but few other life forms can compete with them. It is a difficult decision—now you know why I have four pools! Crayfish are similar; they graze everything vegetarian, but can cohabit with goldfish providing they can hide and find shelter long enough to grow beyond the critical size.

As well as ornamental fish, a number of native fish do very well in a garden pool. Wildlife regulations often place limitations on what can be transported from one water body to another. Check with your local authorities. Local fish are cheaper to replace (though often less colorful) than those from a commercial supplier; this quickly becomes relevant, particularly if a great blue heron or kingfisher discovers your pool!

Pools without fish have the potential for the greatest diversity of wildlife. With fish present, you are unlikely to have salamanders, frogs and many other interesting aquatic species.

What Is a Bug?

To some people, all insects (and spiders too) are bugs! However, bugs, in a strict entomological sense, are well defined. They are insects that have a characteristic "double diamond" pattern when their wings are folded. Bugs are a large, diverse and cosmopolitan group. Common garden pool species include the water boatman, backswimmer, water strider and the giant waterbug that grows to 3 inches (7.5 cm).

Common Aquatic Animals of Garden Pools

Here are some of the animals—insects and non-insects—you would most commonly find in garden pools.

Insects

Mayflies. Habitat: Permanent waters, ponds, lakes and streams.

These 3/4-inch (2-cm) clear-winged flies often dance in unison above the water surface, their long twin or triple tails an identifying feature. Adults do not feed, and they live only a day or two, just long enough to mate and lay their eggs. Mayflies spend the majority of their life cycle as nymphs. Both adult and nymph stages are an important food source for many fish and other aquatic predators.

Dragonflies. Habitat: Permanent waters with shoreline vegetation.

In both adult and nymph stages dragonflies are voracious predators. Nymphs catch all manner of other insects, small fish and tadpoles. Adults feed on small flying insects such as mosquitoes and blackflies. As insects go, dragonflies are large, 2 to 4 inches (5 to 10 cm). Many have brightly colored red, green or blue bodies. Some have brown-patterned wings. The adults are active from late spring until the first really cool weather of autumn.

Damselflies. Habitat: Permanent ponds with aquatic vegetation.

Similar to dragonflies, but smaller and daintier, most damselflies neatly fold their wings over their abdomens. Often they occur in considerable numbers. While some may be red-bodied, most have abdomens patterned sky-blue and black. The nymphs move through the water using a wriggling motion generated by three large, paddle-shaped gills extending from the tip of the abdomen.

The Toe Biter

Also known as the giant water bug, this "true bug" is a formidable predator, often subduing fish as large as itself. It grows to 3 inches (7.5 cm) long. The modified front legs have two strong clasping arms tipped with sharp claws. The mouth has a beak that can inflict a painful sting, hence the name "toe biter." Despite its size, it is also a good flyer. Often, it is attracted to street and porch lights, earning it yet another name—the electric light bug.

Aquatic Bugs. Habitat: Permanent ponds and backwaters.

A variety of bugs are attracted to backyard pools. The aquatic forms have modified legs. The modified back legs of the water-boatman and backswimmer are used like oars. Water striders, which run across the water surface, and water scorpions and giant waterbugs, which swim just below the surface, have front legs that are modified for grasping prey. Most of these species can inflict a painful bite if handled carelessly.

Water Beetles. Habitat: Permanent ponds.

Everyone recognizes a beetle when they see one and water beetles are no exception. Adults swim underwater propelled by an enlarged pair of hind legs that are fringed with hairs to increase their efficiency. Both adults and larvae are highly predacious; the larvae are called "water tigers" on this account. Adults can get to 1 inch long (2.5 cm). See illustration below.

On the surface of quiet ponds and streams you can often spot the gyrating, rapid movements of a group of smaller, black whirligig beetles, which are also predators.

Water Beetle Life Cycle

Pupae (in ground)

Water Tiger

Eggs (laid in water)

Water Beetle

Caddisflies. Habitat: Permanent ponds, streams, lakes and rivers.

The adult caddisfly resembles a medium-sized moth with wings folded like a tent over the abdomen. However, it is not the adults that are most fascinating, it is the larvae, which construct a portable protective case within which they grow. Each species (there are nearly 1,000 in North America) makes a case distinctive in size, shape and materials, which include grains of sand, twigs, needles, snail shells and other objects. Some of these are truly works of art! In pools without large fish, you may see these larvae by the hundreds, grazing on plant material.

Non-Insects

Crayfish. Habitat: Permanent water bodies.

These freshwater crustaceans look like miniature lobsters with large, forward-facing pincers. They are scavengers that feed on whatever plant and animal material is available. Children (both young and old!) enjoy fishing for crayfish using a pole and a short piece of string baited with a piece of meat. The crayfish wraps itself around the bait and can then be lifted slowly to the surface and netted. In many parts of North America the local crayfish (also known as crawdads) are considered a delicacy. Large numbers can graze a pool clean of vegetation. Only large, well-established water lilies will escape these ravages, though their leaves may be well nibbled, even shredded.

Snails and Clams. Habitat: Permanent water bodies, ponds, streams and rivers.

An attractive pool will have a variety of animals living in it. Worthy additions include snails and clams. The red ram's-horn snail is a large, 3/4-inch (2-cm), colorful individual that has been selected for its color. Perhaps the easiest way to acquire this red variety is through a specialty water garden nursery, as finding red ones in the wild may be difficult. The wild populations are generally olive brown, as a protection from predators.

Two other large snails, 1 to 2 inches (3 to 5 cm) in size, that can be collected from local waters are the eared and giant pond snails of the genus *Lymnaea*. The shells of these snails are quite delicate, almost transparent. In the southeastern states the apple snail (North America's largest snail) is a worthy consideration.

North America has quite a number of freshwater mussels, especially in the Mississippi River drainage area. These are

What Is a Mussel?

Mussel is a common name applied to a large number of clams, including both freshwater and saltwater species. Freshwater mussels often have a beautiful pearly luster to the inside of their shells.

large clams, from 1 to 6 inches (2 to 15 cm) in length. They burrow into bottom sediments of a pond or river and remain there, filtering food from the surrounding water. During their mobile larval stage, these mussels are parasitic, attaching themselves to the gills and fins of fish, which allows them to be carried upstream. This habit may be a deterrent to having them in a pond with prize goldfish.

Other Interesting Pond Creatures

Few people are aware that there are freshwater sponges. Not common, these sponges become bright green from an algae that grows within the sponge colony. The sponges form an irregular blob, sometimes 6 inches (15 cm) long which encrusts underwater branches and twigs.

Among the hundreds, if not thousands, of other animals that might find a home in a garden pool, the tiny *Cyclops* and *Daphnia* (a water flea, but not a true flea) are less than pinhead-sized crustaceans.

Mosquito Life Cycle

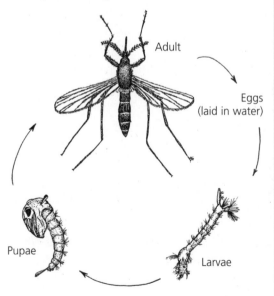

Adult

Eggs
(laid in water)

Pupae

Larvae

Mosquitoes

When talking about garden pools the subject of mosquitoes often comes up. It is tough being a mosquito! Just about every predator found in and around pools eats mosquitoes, making survival very difficult. And should a mosquito survive this gauntlet of enemies, there is hardly a human who would not swat it if given the chance. This is one reason for mosquitoes to have a brief life cycle that utilizes temporary ephemeral pools and puddles as rearing places. Aquatic predators with longer, more complicated life cycles cannot survive in these habitats. You can easily test this fact. Place an ice cream pail of water on your patio or balcony in early spring and see what happens. It is this type of standing water in which most mosquitoes breed— not backyard garden pools.

In their thousands, they make up part of a pool's natural zoo-plankton, important to the food chain.

Constructing a Backyard Pool

A garden pool may range from a natural pond of considerable size to a bathtub sunk into a corner of the garden or a mammoth concrete structure, carefully contoured to fit into the natural terrain. The natural pool takes advantage of local situations where groundwater or a nearby water course is available. All that is required is to dig the pond to the size, shape and depth desired. This depression will then fill naturally with ground water and the water level will fluctuate with the water table. Digging is best done in the dry season. In very wet conditions you may require the use of a backhoe or other earth-moving machinery. Depending on the depth and nature of the soil, sloughing or caving in of the pond's bank could be a problem. It may even go dry.

Not everyone is fortunate enough to have a natural pond on their property, but a variety of materials are now readily available through nurseries, garden shops and building supply companies for those who want to construct a pool on their site.

When building or installing a pool, one of the goals should be to achieve a suitable water depth. It should be deep enough to accommodate water lilies and provide adequate space for fish and aquatic life to move around during winter weather, when the surface might freeze. A good depth is at least 30 inches (75 cm).

Preformed pools using rubber, plastic or fiberglass come in many sizes, shapes and depths. These are simple to install—just dig a basin of the appropriate size and insert the pool. The pool can then be edged with flagstones, brick or other materials to add an attractive touch and a little extra depth. Some people, possibly a little less discriminating (but thrifty) will use an old sink, washtub, bathtub or similar object destined for the local garbage dump. Whatever the source, preformed pools can be made very attractive with appropriate plantings.

While the vertical walls of the formed pools provide greater water depth, the creativity permitted by the free-form method permits shallow areas and islands that are more conducive to wildlife use. Combining both methods will allow your creation to be both practical and aesthetically pleasing.

A pool or pond for wildlife should include areas with different water depths that in turn are planted with a variety of aquatic and semi-aquatic plants. Shallow areas with a gently sloping beach of coarse sand or gravel are used by many insects and birds as drinking stations. The presence of a partly submerged log or a large boulder or two that rises slightly above the surface will serve the same purpose.

Building a Poly Vinyl Chloride (PVC) Pool

Poly vinyl chloride (PVC) is a tough, somewhat elastic plastic material that can stretch with ice pressure and earth settling. The advantage of using PVC liners is that the builder has flexibility in choosing the pool's shape and design. Not to be confused with polyethylene, which hardens and become brittle with age, PVC keeps its original properties and is reported to last as long as concrete.

PVC pool liners come in variety of sizes up to 18 x 25 feet (5.5 x 7.5 m) and can be glued or bonded together so that virtually any size of pool can be created. They are less expensive than concrete and do not require the heavy labor of mixing and pouring cement. All you need do is dig and contour the hole to the desired size and shape, smooth out the bottom and sides to remove any sharp objects that could perforate the liner, insert the liner and fill your new pool. Some effort will be required to touch up the pool's rim to hide the edge of the liner.

Attention needs to be given to allow for overflow during periods of heavy precipitation. There should be a low portion on the pool's rim, constructed in such a manner that soil is not washed away, thereby jeopardizing the pool's overall form. If the liner is held in place (front and back) by a few large stones or concrete blocks to create a spillway, this should suffice.

Further information about installing a PVC pool liner is available from the companies that sell these materials. It is best to talk with them at the planning stage, before you begin construction.

Building a Concrete Pool

Constructing a concrete pool is not as easy as it first might appear. A cubic yard (meter) of wet concrete weighs about 4,400 pounds (2000 kg), so expect some heavy work, even if you plan to use ready-mix delivered by truck! On the plus side, with a good knowledge of the practices required when using concrete, there are few limits to what can be accomplished.

Depending on location, you may need to build a free-form pool that fits into local features and contours. These more natural pools can quite easily be tucked into a chosen location to fit neatly with your garden plan. Because wet cement flows readily, it may be difficult to provide sufficient depth in the center of a small pool to meet the needs of some aquatic plants, especially water lilies. In these circumstances, rock walls or other barriers may be needed to increase the pool's gradient.

A second type of concrete pool uses pre-assembled cement forms into which the wet cement is poured. These forms and their attendant hardware can be rented. Once you get the hang of it, they are quick and easy to set up. Pools built with these forms have vertical walls of geometric shape.

Some Construction Details for a Formed Concrete Pool

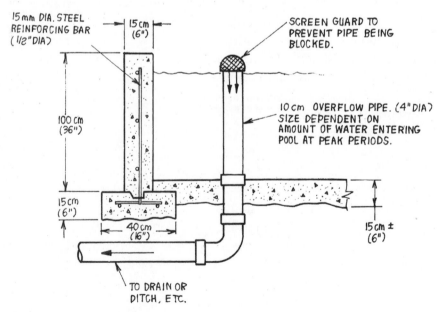

15 mm DIA. STEEL REINFORCING BAR (1/2"DIA)

15 cm (6")

SCREEN GUARD TO PREVENT PIPE BEING BLOCKED.

10 cm OVERFLOW PIPE. (4"DIA) SIZE DEPENDENT ON AMOUNT OF WATER ENTERING POOL AT PEAK PERIODS.

100 cm (36")

15 cm (6")

40 cm (16")

15 cm ± (6")

TO DRAIN OR DITCH, ETC.

Small butterflies of many species love oregano (page 10).

Swallowtail caterpillars are large and colorful. Larval food plants (page 11) are important for enhancing garden butterfly populations.

A Western swallowtail feeding on nectar from red valerian flowers (pages 10 and 16).

Caddisflies are among a variety of aquatic insects that will complete their life cycle in a garden pool. Their larvae build elaborate homes to protect their abdomen (page 33).

Large dragonflies, often called darners, are predators of small flying insects around garden ponds (page 32).

Dragonfly nymph cases are often found on riparian vegetation (page 32).

True to their name, tree frogs spend much of their time basking and hunting in poolside vegetation (page 45).

Skinks are one of our more common lizards. They enjoy soft sandy soils with boulders and light vegetation cover (page 55).

Black raspberry, also known as 'Blackcap', is a good fruit producer (page 132).

The berries of the red elderberry are a favorite food of the western band-tailed pigeon (page 137).

Native cherries, like this chokecherry, are favored feeding sites for fruit eating birds and mammals (page 104).

Water lilies are available in many colorful forms that add beauty to garden pools (page 41).

Every pond should have a turtle (page 55). Pictured here is one of the author's ponds shortly after construction (page 30).

Garden pools can be an attractive addition to a backyard or front yard (page 30).

Butterflies enjoy small tubular flowers like those of red valerian also know as Jupiter's Beard (page 16).

A very attractive patio/balcony garden, utilizing a variety of colorful plants (page 117).

A lovely window box filled with flowering plants (page 118).

Squirrels and chipmunks are active daytime mammals that are easily attracted to feeding stations (pages 63-64).

Bird houses for swallows or bluebirds if placed in forest settings will be adapted for use by flying squirrels (page 65). Note the teeth marks around the entrance hole.

Keeping large birds away from a peanut food source can be accomplished in a number of ways (page 102).

Pyracantha hedges due to their stiff tangles of spiny branches are good barriers and property delineators (page 136). Their fruits are eagerly sought by winter birds.

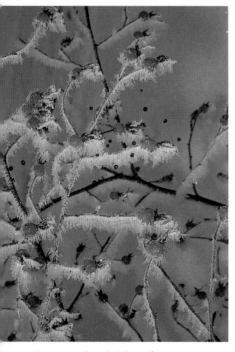

Winter rose hips brighten frosty mornings (page 137).

Poles placed against a tree or upright posts are ideal hibernation sites for butterflies (page 19) as well as protection for mammals and small birds.

Yet a third type of cement pool construction uses a cement product that is sprayed onto steep surfaces and reinforced by rebar (reinforcing steel) or heavy mesh. This process allows great versatility in designing the pool, but specialized equipment and expertise is required. Professional cement contractors are the best source for further information on this construction method.

All cement walls will eventually develop cracks, no matter how well built they are. To minimize cracking and maintain strength over the long term, the use of rebar is a *must*. With proper construction methods most cracks will be small and will only weep. Often they will plug up naturally, but a little good-quality clay rubbed over the crack, on the inside surface, will help hasten this process.

When building a formed pool, either the floor, or footing to support the wall, should be poured first. Because pools are likely to freeze in winter, ½-inch (15-mm) steel reinforcing bars should be used both horizontally and vertically at about 20-inch (50-cm) intervals to prevent or reduce cracking. Make sure there is a continuous key-way, or groove, in the footings or floor perimeter. When the walls are poured, this will provide a snug, watertight fit.

Never underestimate the strength of wet cement. If your forms pull apart you are in for a terrible amount of grief. Don't hesitate to consult or obtain advice from a local contractor or cement expert. They can provide you with information that could make your job easier and your pool more attractive.

Curing a Cement Pool

Free lime that leaches from new concrete is quite toxic to plants, fish and other aquatic life. Filling and flushing your new

Fishing Spiders

Of the spider species that are found in and around ponds, the fishing spiders (*Dolomedes* species) are perhaps the most interesting. A fishing spider can dive and remain submerged for prolonged periods. Although it feeds primarily on insects, it has been observed to catch small fish and tadpoles. It is a fairly large, brown spider, about ¾-inch (1.5 cm) with a pair of light highlights on the body.

pool three or four times at intervals of at least 24 hours will remove most of the lime. On the last rinse, allow the water to stand for a week. Then all should be safe.

Sources of Pool Water

In natural ponds, seasonal fluctuations in the groundwater table can be quite dramatic; some ponds may even dry out completely in most summers. Some animals, like fairy shrimp, actually require that their pond dry out between generations. Their eggs and cocoons, baked into the bottom sediments, will hatch with the next heavy rains. But most freshwater species of plants and animals prefer a relatively stable water level, and a full pond is also much more appealing to the eye than one with a low water level.

The very fortunate wildlife gardener will have a natural spring or small permanent water course on the property. But more likely it will be the garden hose that provides water for your pool. The roof of your house is a water catchment and by simply directing one or more downspouts to your pool it could provide all the water you need. Tap water can top up the pool in dry weather. As long as you do not add too much at once, any adverse effects from chlorination or other water treatments should be minimal. Chlorine is a gas, so it dissipates quickly, even more so when it is dripped into a broad, shallow birdbath that overflows into the pool. Water as a byproduct of an air conditioning system is another consideration.

Providing for Overflow and Drainage

To keep your pool from overflowing into your garden, install a good drainage system. (See illustration page 38) The overflow pipe, cut to the desired length, should friction-fit snugly into the appropriate coupling cemented into the pool's floor. This overflow will also act as a safety release in case of a sudden flood or when a good clean-out is required. Fitting the opening with a coarse screen, as indicated, will prevent it from getting plugged by large objects, though it may be prone to clogging by smaller objects.

Care and Maintenance of the Garden Pool

Once a pool and its plant and animal life becomes a balanced unit, annual care and maintenance should be minimal. Each spring and/or fall, remove excess organic matter, such as fallen leaves, needles and dead stalks of the previous season's growth. This will prolong the periods between major cleanings.

Loss of water clarity is usually an indication that something is out of balance. Excessive amounts of dead vegetation, or too much fish food or fertilizer are often the primary problems. Clean the pool and replace the water.

Pools, particularly those with fish, frogs or tadpoles, are meccas for curious children. Never forget public safety when young children are about.

Some Common Native Plants Suitable for Garden Pools

A tremendous number of plants have been cultivated over the past century. Just look at the selection of water lilies. You can get virtually every flower color imaginable, from violet to white. This is exciting! Local specialist nurseries have information on water plants that will add color and diversity to your pool, but do not forget that local marshes or ponds contain interesting native plants. These are already acclimatized to your growing conditions and may be available for the taking, once you have received permission from the landowner.

The following chart lists some wide-ranging native plants with interesting qualities that make them worthy of a place in or around most pools. Bladderwort is truly fascinating. Although the yellow flower is attractive, the tiny bladders that keep the leaves

Sundew in a Pot

Sundew is a fascinating little plant of peat bogs. Its leaves have long glandular hairs crowned with knobs of sweet sticky liquid. Insects up to the size of damselflies that alight on the leaves are trapped in the liquid and eventually digested. Sundew grows well in garden pools. Fill a large pot with peat moss (or better still, live sphagnum moss), and place the pot so the rim rises 2 to 3 inches (5 cm) above the surface. Both the long-leaved (*Drosera anglica*) and round-leaved (*Drosera rotundifolia*) sundew thrive in this environment. Both produce a spike of small white flowers.

afloat are more interesting. Each bladder, just ⅛-inch (2 to 3 mm) long, is also a minuscule trap for catching minute pond animals that the plant digests to acquire nitrogen.

Of the two water lilies listed, *Nymphaea* is the pick for color and general attractiveness. There are many species of pondweeds with a multitude of forms, but just about all have both submerged and floating leaves that are quite different in shape and form. Some grow to be more than 7 feet (2 m) long. The flower spike is small and dull brown or green. Water smartweed is similar, but has a bright pink, thumb-sized cluster of flowers held slightly above the surface.

Most of the submerged oxygenators listed below have found their way into the home aquarium trade, particularly fanwort and wild celery. Once established, as is the case with many pond plants, you will have to thin the plants and remove the excess.

A general rule of thumb to help determine the number of plants required for your pool is one water lily and three bunches of pondweeds (*Elodea*, *Cabomba*, *Potamogeton*, etc.) per square yard (meter) of pond surface, for the portions of your pool more than or 2½ feet (75 cm) deep.

It will take the vegetation in your pool a year or two grow in and fill out into a balanced system. Once established, you will probably need to control their spread by regular thinning. Healthy surplus plants can be given to friends, traded or possibly turned in for credit at your local nursery.

Purple Loosestrife (Lythrum salicaria)

Though beautiful, this Eurasian species has become a nasty pest, responsible for choking out many native plants and overrunning considerable wetland areas. It has been described as the "beautiful killer" and gardeners should not bring it into their gardens. Once established, it is very difficult to eradicate.

Floating plants
- Duckweed (*Lemna minor*)
- Bladderwort (*Utricularia* species)

Deep-water plants with floating leaves 2 to 4 feet (60 to 120 cm) deep
- Pondweeds (*Potamogeton* species)
- Water lilies (*Nuphar* species and *Nymphaea* species)
- Watershield (*Brasenia* species)

Deep-water submerged oxygenators
- Canada waterweed (*Elodea canadensis*)
- Water-milfoil (*Myriophyllum* species)
- Fanwort (*Cabomba* species)
- Wild celery (*Vallisneria* species)

Shallow water plants 1 foot (30 cm) deep
- Cattail (*Typha* species)
- Hardstem bulrush (*Scirpus acutus*)
- Pickerel weed (*Pontederia cordata*)
- Arrowhead (Wapato) (*Sagittaria* species)
- Water plantain (*Alisma plantago-aquatica*)
- Buck bean (*Menyanthes trifoliata*)
- Yellow iris (*Iris pseudacorus*)
- Marsh cinquefoil (*Potentilla palustris*)
- Water smartweed (*Polygonum coccineum*)
- Aquatic buttercups (*Ranunculus aquatilis* and other buttercup species)

Emergent and shoreline plants
Perennials
- Blue iris (*Iris* species)
- Yellow loosestrife (*Lysimachia* species)
- Cardinal flower (*Lobelia cardinalis*)
- Skullcaps (*Scutellaria* species)
- Water-parsley (*Oenanthe sarmentosa*)
- Forget-me-nots (*Myosotis* species)
- Sundew (*Drosera* species)
Shrubs
- Meadowsweet (*Spiraea alba*)
- Douglas's spirea (*Spiraea douglasii*)
- Sweet gale (*Myrica gale*)
- Red-osier dogwood (*Cornus sericea*)
- Willows (*Salix* species)

Cattail or Bulrush

Distinguishing a cattail (pictured above) from a bulrush is really quite easy once you understand you are dealing with two distinct entities. The confusion exists because these names are often used interchangeably. Cattail (*Typha*) is the flat-leaved plant whose flower head forms the familiar brown club. Bulrush (*Scirpus*), sometimes called tule, has tall cylindrical stems with a tassel of small brown flower clusters. Both cattail and bulrush species are suitable for the garden pool. Cattail has the added advantage of its flower heads producing a high-quality nesting material for birds.

CHAPTER 5
Gardening for Amphibians

Gardening for amphibians is an interesting challenge. The key to success for these largely damp-skinned animals is moisture. In their adult stages, all are predatory carnivores and for this reason alone are to be valued. Their economic benefit to humans has been described as incalculable. In many environments, for their numbers and in weight per acre, amphibians, particularly salamanders, often place #1 for biomass! And yet, despite their incredible numbers, we seldom see them, as most remain hidden by day.

In the evolutionary picture, amphibians are intermediate between fish and reptiles. While many species coexist with fish and a few, like the spade-foot toad, live alongside some of the reptiles in drier environments, most amphibians are found in moist terrestrial habitats with high humidity and moderate temperatures. This habitat, devoid of fish and most reptiles, amphibians share with birds and mammals.

Salamanders and frogs are cold-blooded, deriving their body temperature from the environment where they live. This largely accounts for their slow movement, frogs being an exception. Although some have lungs, most respiration takes place through the skin. Many aquatic forms and most tadpoles and salamander larvae have gills for breathing. Some salamanders are totally terrestrial, while others are capable of completing their entire life cycle in an aquatic larval form. Most small amphibians have a life expectancy of three to five years, frogs slightly longer than salamanders.

In recent years concerns have been raised about declining amphibian populations, particularly frogs. The reasons for this apparent decline are not clear, though fingers point to habitat destruction and possibly to air and water quality changes. Urban areas, where domestic and feral cats and dogs abound, further challenge survival and reproduction of amphibians.

Many people place frogs and salamanders low on the list of favorite species. More often, this fascinating group of animals is simply neglected. In my garden, the first chirp of a tree frog brings considerable glee, and the chorus that follows is greatly enjoyed.

In North America we have nearly 200 amphibian species, with a few more salamander species than frogs and toads. Extreme dryness and cold limit their distribution. The Gulf States record about 60 species, Alaska only six! Most gardens of reasonable extent and appropriate habitat can become a home to one or more species of amphibians, but special care is required to ensure their survival.

Large gardens with a good-sized, well-vegetated pool might well be able to support a small frog or salamander population. Getting these species started will often require bringing in the appropriate local species, in the form of egg masses. Young will imprint on their surroundings and will likely become permanent residents.

Some Common Garden Amphibians

Tree Frogs, Spring Peepers

Habitat: Marshy ponds with emergent vegetation.

These are a group of about 30 species of small, cryptically colored frogs. They include the tree frogs, spring peepers, cricket frogs and chorus frogs, which first herald the coming of spring. Once their choruses are underway we know spring is about to arrive. As the males make their way to their natal ponds, the chorus

A "True" Frog

"True" and "typical" are general terms that have meaning to those with extensive experience in a particular area of study. Herpetologists, people who are experts on reptiles and amphibians, have determined that the typical, or most frog-like, frogs are the members of the family Ranidae to which our leopard frogs and bullfrogs belong. These frogs have a bony breastbone and horizontal pupils. Ours are large frogs, often with a conspicuous ear membrane, or tympanum.

grows and soon the females follow. These are the frogs that *ribbet-ribbet-ribbet*, all night long. Only the males sing, and the only thing that quiets their revelry is our approach—or so it seems.

Many of these species are the "sticky-toed" frogs that have an enlarged adhesive pad at the tip of each toe. With these toe tips they can stick to almost everything, and can climb vertical glass surfaces with ease.

It is the tadpoles, or pollywogs, of these species that children most often bring home. Watching their transformation from tadpoles to tiny frogs is a fascinating science lesson.

In garden pools these small frogs can do very well, sometimes even becoming a bit of a nuisance. By late spring their chorusing will have ceased, but their small gelatinous spawn clusters can be seen attached to pool vegetation. By midsummer, tiny frogs, this year's cohort of survivors, will start to make their way into nearby vegetation where they press tightly against leaves. Their task now is to survive until their first breeding season, the following spring.

Leopard Frogs

Habitat: Larger ponds and marshes.

These medium-sized frogs are what scientists consider to be "true" frogs. About 16 species of similar appearance are in this group, which is distributed across North America. Most are southern inhabitants, but the wood frog extends almost all the way to the Arctic Ocean. Some have no mating calls and others use grunts, quacks and clucks—none particularly musical. Their spawn is laid in large, grapefruit-sized and larger masses that eventually float and spread out on the surface.

Leopard frogs can be identifed by their spotted coloration and jumping prowess. When frightened, they make their escape in long, zigzag leaps. Garden pools are probably not the ideal habitat for leopard frogs, though transients may appear from time to time.

Telling Male From Female Tree Frogs

Every kid should be able to separate a "boy" tree frog from a "girl" tree frog. As it is the males that do the singing, they are the ones with the elastic inflatable throat pouch that is olive to dark brown in color. Female tree frogs tend to be larger, and their throats are almost white.

Bullfrogs

Habitat: Large, deep-water ponds.

This huge eastern frog has been widely introduced to areas outside its normal range, primarily to be "farmed" for the frog leg market. When these attempts were abandoned, the frogs became naturalized and their populations dispersed. Today, in many western locations bullfrogs have become serious predators of smaller native frogs and other edible species, including ducklings and blackbirds.

The bullfrog is another "true" frog. One distinguishing feature is its huge tadpoles, which reach 5 inches (12 cm) in length and take up to three years to metamorphose into their adult form. Bullfrogs, like other true frogs, have large, conspicuous tympanums (ear membranes). They often emit a "meow" call when leaping into water. They are very wary by day but are more easily approached at night. Under a beam of light, their eyes, like those of many other animals, reflect back light known as an eyeshine. Often they can easily be approached and caught in this manner.

Toads

Habitat: Dry habitats with places to burrow or hide and access to moisture for breeding.

The common toads (*Bufo*) and the spadefoot toads (*Scaphiopus*) are our most common species. Both have granular or warty skin. In the true toads the warts and the prominent parotid glands behind the head are poisonous. The poisons have been known to kill dogs and snakes that have tried to eat these animals. After handling toads, it is a good idea to wash one's hands.

Toads are the tortoises of the amphibians—they are adapted to live in dry environments, but they must find ponds or temporary puddles for egg laying and tadpole development. For the spadefoots,

Frog Choruses

One of the wonderful natural events each spring is the frog chorus. Each species has a distinct call and preferred ponds where the males gather to vocalize. Some calls are quick and cricket-like, some are a long grumble lasting a few seconds. The bullfrog's call is a deep reverberating *jug-a-rum*. These calls are easily recognizable with practice. An intriguing phenomenon is the sudden mantle of silence that crisply falls at the slightest hint of a prowler or predator.

Children—and adults—enjoy imitating the sound of the singers to induce the frogs to resume calling.

heavy rains that create temporary pools trigger breeding. In dry years, spadefoots may never breed at all. Due to the ephemeral nature of their breeding pools, spadefoots have a speedy transition from egg to tadpole to terrestrial sub-adult. It can be as short as 12 to 13 days—the shortest of any known frog or toad.

The spadefoots are appropriately named. A horny spur on the inside of each hind foot assists digging and burrowing in sandy soil. Another unique feature of this group is the vertical pupil opening in their eyes.

True toads lay their eggs in long double strings, and toad tadpoles tend to be black, distinguishing them from the brown tadpoles of frogs.

Toad Lights

Garden lighting systems attract nighttime flying and terrestrial insects that can quickly become toad food. Just like the gecko (lizards) of tropical environments, toads will often gather to feed around light sources. As the insects arrive, they are quickly gobbled up!

Both groups are nocturnal foragers that emerge at night to hunt insects. Toad lights, to attract insects, and toad holes to provide daytime hideaways are two methods of bringing these amphibians into your garden.

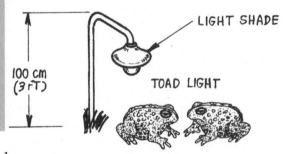

LIGHT SHADE

100 CM
(3 FT)

TOAD LIGHT

Aquatic Salamanders

Habitat: Permanent water bodies with moist soft ground adjacent.

Salamanders fall into two groups, those that are totally terrestrial and breed on land and those that require ponds, pools or lakes in which to lay their eggs. Salamanders are silent. Their slow movements and preference for cracks, crevices and caverns, out of sight, often gives little indication of their presence. Unless you make a reasonably diligent search, you almost have to stumble upon them to know they are present. Gardeners occasionally find them, but generally they remain elusive.

Tiger and mole salamanders (*Ambystoma* species) and mudpuppies and waterdogs (*Necturus* species) are among the aquatic group.

During their aquatic stage, these species have large plumose gills that distinguish them from frog tadpoles. When they become terrestrial (for example, the tiger and some mole salamanders), they lose these breathing structures. Some, like mudpuppies and waterdogs, are totally aquatic, remaining and breeding in their larval form. Mudpuppies can grow to 18 inches (45 cm).

Aquatic species lay their eggs in masses similar in size and shape to those of frogs. Upon hatching, they resemble miniature adults with four legs and a long tail. Depending on their genetic destiny, most will transform into adults and leave their natal ponds to forage in nearby moist habitats.

The largest and perhaps most striking of our salamanders is the tiger salamander, which is found from eastern Washington to the Great Lakes. They live near water under natural debris or in the burrows of other animals. The adults and larvae often become more than a foot (30 cm) long with colorful black and yellow markings. The tiger salamander is a voracious animal, consuming earthworms, large insects, other amphibians and even small mice.

Garden pools offer good breeding habitats for many of these species. Those that are completely aquatic will need to be imported to get them started. Nearby habitats can be improved for adult salamanders by providing rock and wood piles that are kept moist during periods of dry weather.

Long-Toed Salamander Life Cycle

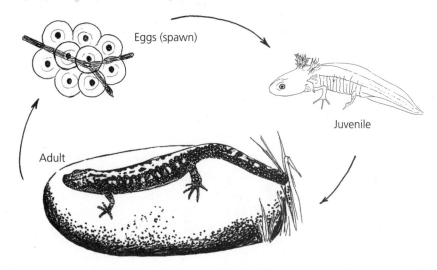

Eggs (spawn)

Juvenile

Adult

Terrestrial Salamanders

Habitat: Moist woodlands with lots of leaf litter and downed wood.

Red-backed salamander

This is our largest salamander group, with about 25 species. These salamanders do not need water for breeding purposes. They spend virtually their entire lives beneath forest litter, often within rotting logs. Mole salamanders are often mottled with yellow. Woodland salamanders have short legs and often have reddish or mustard markings.

They are most often found by accident when landscaping requires the movement of rocks, boulders and larger woody debris. When stacked firewood becomes damp, these salamanders often find their way into the pile. If you know you have salamanders in the vicinity of your garden, you can encourage them by providing this type of habitat around the periphery.

Newts

Habitat: Undisturbed terrestrial habitats close to water sources for breeding.

Newts are the third type of salamander commonly found in North America. Newts have a granular rather than smooth skin. Like the skin of toads, it contains some powerful poisons. People have died from swallowing western newts, but this should not deter us from encouraging them in our gardens. The eastern newt is found from southern Canada south, but generally east of the Mississippi River. The western species generally hug the west coast.

The life histories of these two groups are somewhat different. Both lay their eggs singly in nearby water bodies. A few months after hatching, the larvae transform into young newts. In the eastern species these immatures are called efts and differ from the adults in being orange

Frog Spawn/ Salamander Spawn

Many amphibians lay their eggs in distinctive, easily recognizable bunches. Toads' eggs are in long strings. Northwestern salamanders produce relatively firm, oval, grapefruit-sized balls. Newts lay their eggs singly, and tree frogs lay small loose masses 1½ to 3 inches (3 to 7 cm) in diameter.

to red in color. After a year or more of a terrestrial existence they become greenish-brown adults and return to the water where they remain. In the western species, the immatures resemble miniature adults. After egg laying, western newts return to a terrestrial existence, where they remain until the next breeding season.

Gardens for Amphibians

Amphibians will use pools that have adequate depth and a reasonable assortment of aquatic and emergent vegetation. The absence of predators such as goldfish and crayfish is, however, a must. (See Chapter 4 for more information about constructing and maintaining an attractive garden pool.)

Most amphibians move away from pools once their breeding season is over. Areas that maintain a moist, cool, damp environment become their habitat for the remainder of the year. Rock piles, wood piles, stumps, rotting logs with loose bark and their associated debris are good amphibian habitats, particularly for salamanders. If these don't occur naturally, they can easily be created around the periphery of a garden.

Tree frogs and a number of the other frog species are much more mobile. Some will continue their existence in nearby foliage while others will move considerable distances to seek out water courses and lake shores. Toads, not as mobile as frogs, seek shelter or burrow into the ground where they rest during

Toad Holes

Common and spadefoot toads are both relatively dry-skinned, an adaptation to drier environments. To escape high daytime temperatures they seek out shelter, often by burrowing into the ground. Artificial burrows, 2 to 4 inches (5 to 10 cm) in diameter and 12 to 18 inches (30 to 45 cm) deep can be built into most gardens quite easily. Soft, fine sand at the bottom of these tunnels makes an ideal retreat.

Construction Details of a Toad Hole

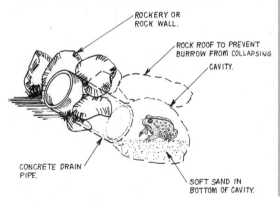

ROCKERY OR ROCK WALL.

ROCK ROOF TO PREVENT BURROW FROM COLLAPSING.

CAVITY.

CONCRETE DRAIN PIPE.

SOFT SAND IN BOTTOM OF CAVITY.

the heat of the day. At night they become active again when they forage for food.

Each year I purchase a cord or two of firewood and invariably a few rotten lengths make their way into this purchase. These are accepted without fuss and added to a corner of the property to enhance salamander habitat. During the drier months of July and August this corner is given one or two good soakings with a hose to ensure it does not dry out too badly.

CHAPTER 6
Gardening for Reptiles

Garden settings are not the most beneficial habitats for many of North America's 280 or so species of reptiles. Urban daytime environments with dogs, cats and cars make their long-term survival difficult. Road shoulders and paved roads are ideal basking sites that often lure reptiles into unsafe situations. Nonetheless, a number of lizards, snakes, turtles and tortoises will find a reasonably sized garden with a diversity of terrains suitable to their needs.

Like amphibians, reptiles are cold-blooded, but their diurnal rather than nocturnal habits allow us to come in contact with them more regularly. Reptiles are quick-moving and this, combined with their habit of sunbathing, can give us a real fright when we disturb them unexpectedly. With the changing of season from summer to autumn, reptiles retire underground to escape the cold. Here they remain dormant for a number of months, awaiting the warmth of spring.

Reptiles have evolved beyond the amphibians in a number of ways. Their dependence upon water is much reduced, allowing them to move into drier habitats. Like a few of the salamanders, they lay their eggs or give birth to live young on dry land. Newborn reptiles resemble miniature adults—their larval, or pollywog, stage is passed while inside the egg. Even though they have lost their strong dependence on water, many species, particularly the turtles and a number of the snakes, are closely associated with ponds, water courses and marshy environments.

In their diet, reptiles are specialized and selective, concentrating on a small number of prey organisms. The horned lizard, as an example, feeds on ants. Most reptiles are carnivorous, but a few are omnivorous, having both plant and animal material in their diet.

If a gardener accepts the concept that a good wildlife garden should meld with surrounding natural environments, then the periphery of this garden oasis can become ideal reptile habitat. Features such as rock and brush piles can often be located here, tucked away or concealed behind a screen of shrubbery. In these places our common reptiles will feel most at home. As with all aspects of wildlife gardening, a little thought and planning to incorporate these features into your garden plan will go a long way to making these cold-blooded animals part of your backyard wildlife menagerie.

Lizard Tails

There are several animals that can regenerate lost body parts. Among these are a number of lizards. It is often hard to find skinks or alligator lizards with a perfect tail.

As a defense mechanism these species have the ability to release a portion or nearly all of their tail when it has been grabbed. The predator is left with a wriggling tail while the lizard quickly disappears. The stump regenerates a new tip, but this will never be quite as well formed as the one that was lost.

Alligator lizard—note the regenerated tail.

Common Garden Reptiles

Reptiles fall into four easily recognized groups; alligators and crocodiles; lizards; snakes; and turtles and tortoises. All have a dry scaly skin (plates or shields in turtles) and most of those that have legs, have stout, strong toenails. Here are some common, wide-ranging species that might find their way or be suitable for importation into a garden setting.

Reptile	Needs	Comments
Pond turtles (*Clemmys* species)	Well-vegetated ponds or pools with water cress and other aquatic plants.	The most aquatic of our turtles; likes to bask on logs and cattail mats, etc.
Painted turtles (*Chrysemys* species)	Deep pools or ponds with a muddy bottom for hibernation.	More carnivorous than the pond turtle. Often has an orange belly with dark markings. Males have long toenails.
Box turtles (*Terrapene* species)	Open spaces with sandy soils for burrows.	Digs burrows for shelter. Activity is stimulated by rain. Feeds on insects, berries and young shoots.
Fence lizards (*Sceloporus* species)	Areas with rock and brush piles for sunning and cover.	Often suns on fence posts and buildings. Males have a blue throat—hence the name "blue belly."
Horned lizards (*Phrynosoma* species)	Open areas with fine soft sand and ant nests.	Better known as horned toads on account of their shape and horn-like head projections.
Skinks (*Eumeces* species)	Sunny areas with leaf litter, logs, rocks and soft soils.	Beautiful small lizards, often with bright blue tails. Many are handsomely striped.
Alligator lizards (*Gerrhonotus* species)	Rock piles and rocky vegetated hillsides.	Western species that may attempt to bite when grasped. Tails break off easily.
Green anole (*Anolis carolinensis*)	Warm climates with lots of vegetation.	The American chameleon has the ability to change color. Males have a red dewlap that they can puff out.
Garter snakes (*Thamnophis* species)	Sunny exposed banks and garden edges; enjoy water sources such as pools.	Many with beautiful coloration. Beneficial— often feed on slugs.

Turtles and Tortoises

Turtles are the best known and appreciated of reptiles. Many people have had pet turtles at one time or another, and extending this interest to a garden pool—or garden, in the case of tortoises—is natural.

Turtles are the amphibious members of the group. A good-sized, deep pool with a soft or muddy bottom will allow them to live outdoors all year round. If you have native turtles in your vicinity, these are the species that should be considered for your pool. The pet-store turtles (often the red-eared or pond slider) are largely southern turtles that do not do well outside their normal ranges.

Turtles are natural predators of fish, crayfish and aquatic insects. Fancy fish and turtles do not mix. Many turtles have a considerable vegetable component in their diet, making aquatic plants a valuable part of their fare. They can be induced to take food from your hand with a little training.

Tortoises, on the other hand, are almost completely terrestrial. They are prone to wandering off in search of their food needs. To keep them within our gardens (and turtles close to their pools) a good fence or other type of barrier will probably be required. Supplemental feeding and either an artificial burrow or a place where your tortoise can dig its own burrow will be required. As with turtles, if you have a native species of tortoise living in your area, then this is the species you should consider.

There is a place in almost every garden for a turtle or tortoise, providing the environment is suitable. Many well-known gardens have had famous reptile residents. The Tongan royal residence in Nukualofa had Tui Malila, a Madagascar tortoise, allegedly given to the royal family by Captain Cook. If this is true (and there is reason to be suspicious), when Tui Malila died in 1966, this tortoise would have been almost 200 years old! Whatever its age, this makes for a good story and provides every gardener with the possibility of continuing the tradition of having a pet garden tortoise.

Lizards

North America has a nice assortment of lizards but most are seldom found in urban areas. In the Carolinas, Florida and the Gulf

States, the green anole or chameleon (not the "true" chameleon of Africa) is seen almost anywhere there are tangles of vegetation. Most of the other species mentioned in the chart are wide-ranging; many penetrate far north, some crossing into Canada.

All of these, with the exception of horned lizards, which like sandy soils for burrowing, require sunny exposed places to bask. Rock and brush piles, logs, rough posts and similar debris make ideal sunning locations. All are insect predators.

Preferred habitats for skinks usually have soft or sandy ground where they can dig or borrow under rocks. Alligator lizards are more at home in rock piles and talus slopes.

Like the turtles and tortoises, these species lay eggs (except alligator lizards, which give birth to live young). A warm, open location with soft soils is the usual repository for their eggs.

Our common lizards provide an interesting addition to any garden. Most are sedentary, having preferred areas that they frequent. The ones listed are relatively small, wide-ranging species. Predators, especially cats, appear to be the limiting factor that prevents lizards from maintaining viable populations in suburban areas, especially gardens.

Snakes

Snakes are often considered the most loathsome of creatures. Many people are downright terrified of *any* snake, even the most harmless varieties. This ingrained fear is unfortunate, a sad commentary on our view of a very interesting and beneficial group of animals. Garter snakes, for instance, are major predators of slugs. Other species are major predators of rats and mice. The backyard gardener should consider these snakes to be prized allies, rather than despised trespassers.

North America has a fairly rich snake fauna, approximately 115 species. Most are southern and eastern in their distribution. Some are *very* poisonous, but the 13 species of garter snake are benign and these are the species most gardeners will come in contact with.

Garter snakes generally prefer locations with a warm, sunny exposure and ample places to retreat and hide. After cool damp spells of weather, they love to find low-level perches in full sun.

Most garter snakes enjoy partially aquatic environments. In garden settings, edges, banks, fish ponds, ditches and semi-wild areas are favored garter snake habitats. They are also surprisingly adept as underwater predators of small fish, frogs, tadpoles and salamander larvae. They frequently adopt a pool and remain in residence until the local food supply is diminished.

Snakeskins

One of the intriguing aspects of snakes and lizards is the ability to shed their skins. For snakes the entire skin comes off in one molting. Finding a complete snake skin and keeping it in one piece is a delicate operation but can net you a natural curiosity.

Snakes about to molt show one telltale sign—their eyes become cloudy! (See photo.) At this time they are virtually blind. A snake's cornea is part of its skin and is shed during each molt. Next time you find a snake's skin, look for the eye. Snakes often molt two or more times a year.

During the winter months most snakes hibernate in subterranean dens called hibernacula. Such dens can be provided for in rock walls, rockeries or hillsides by allowing adequate space between the rocks and boulders used as building materials. The depth of these structures should approach 40 inches (1 m) so that the denning sites remain above the winter water table to prevent flooding.

Garter snake ready to moult.

CHAPTER 7
Gardening for Small Mammals

Years ago, a house we purchased came complete with a large, active colony of carpenter ants, which was munching its way through the timbers behind the kitchen sink. These ants had their access or exit on the outside wall near the sill. From this opening they made forays into the garden to quench their thirst. Their crunching noise in the wall was obvious and somewhat perturbing, but due to the magnitude of the problem and difficulty of repair, not to mention a personal prejudice against chemical extermination, procrastination was the order of the day.

As spring passed into summer, the ants' activity, rather than increasing, began to diminish. Along the nearby footpath we began to find small scats tightly packed with second-hand ant skeletons. Thank goodness none of us stumbled upon the animal responsible, but the skunk or family of skunks provided enough biological control so that the once-thriving ant colony foundered and was never again a problem.

This solution was an unexpected and educational sidelight to the enjoyment of rural, backyard wildlife. Would it not be nice if all problems with cohabiting wildlife could be solved by simple inaction!

In an urban or garden setting, the smaller mammals are often attracted for the wrong reasons. Raccoons, skunks and opossums can become nuisance animals that get into garbage or find their way into places where they are not wanted. More often than not, these situations are a sad commentary, not on the animals but on a generally sloppy and careless lifestyle. It is most often the animals that come off second-best, when really it is not their fault.

One of the primary cornerstones of wildlife gardening must be that the gardener feels secure that what he or she is trying to accomplish will not cause damage to personal property or be injurious to health. (Chapter 16 deals with a number of questions around this issue.)

Being able to watch mammals from a secure and safe viewpoint is a particularly rewarding event. In a backyard setting, this can be a frustrating challenge. First, most of these species, aside from the squirrels and chipmunks, are rather secretive, using the cover of darkness to conceal their presence. They are also quiet. Second, due to their size and habits they are often the first species to fall prey to or be harassed by local cats and dogs. Taking these considerations into account, it will be the exceptional rather than average garden that can successfully cater to small mammals.

Once raccoons, opossums, skunks or flying squirrels have found a feeding station, however, they will return with regularity. During the day, squirrels and chipmunks will do the same. Where surplus food remains available, unfortunately rats and house mice can become unwanted guests. Ridding garden areas of these rodents can be quite a challenge.

Not all garden mammals are terrestrial. Flying squirrels and bats are more common than most people would believe. To appreciate

Small Mammal or Raccoon Roost Box

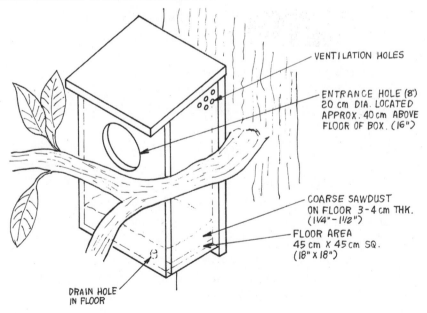

VENTILATION HOLES

ENTRANCE HOLE (8")
20 cm DIA. LOCATED
APPROX. 40 cm ABOVE
FLOOR OF BOX. (16")

COARSE SAWDUST
ON FLOOR 3-4 cm THK.
(1¼" - 1½")

FLOOR AREA
45 cm X 45 cm SQ.
(18" X 18")

DRAIN HOLE
IN FLOOR

their presence, knowing when to look is almost as important as where to look. Just after dusk, these animals venture forth—flying squirrels to bird feeders, bats to nearby ponds and pools for a drink.

Many mammals require a space to den up over the winter or raise their offspring. These are the times when garden sheds, garages, greenhouses, spaces under buildings and even attics are sought out. The presence of sleeping or nursing animals is usually benign, but not without risk. Providing a location for these activities away from human habitations is prudent. See pages 60 and 64 for a rough plan for these structures.

Small mammals may not be the easiest garden wildlife to observe or the easiest to cater to, but species for species, they offer one of the best entertainment values!

Some Garden-Frequenting Mammals

Virginia Opossums

Habitat: Denning sites, hollow logs or trees, old burrows, brush piles.

Opossums are generally solitary, nocturnal animals. The opossum is North America's only marsupial. The female gives birth to tiny, 3/4-inch-long (15-mm) young that find their way into her pouch, or marsupium, where they remain for more than two months. The litters are large, with an average size of eight to nine. Two litters per year, one in late winter and another in late spring, is not unusual. Opossums can live up to seven years. They are good swimmers and climbers, the latter assisted by their prehensile tail.

One of the opossum's best-known habits, feigning death, is believed to be brought on by shock. This, combined with a strong disagreeable odor, gives the opossum a degree of protection from predators. Its main enemy is the automobile, due to its slow gait in crossing roads at night. Opossums are highly resistant to rabies.

The opossum is an oddity in a backyard garden. It has very broad food tastes, so it can be a nuisance in vegetable gardens and orchards, but is also known to eat noxious insects.

Cottontail Rabbits

Habitat: Dense thickets and hedgerows near food meadows.

Rabbits, like opossums, have to be prolific as they are main prey species for many predators, such as owls and foxes. In urban environments, rabbits can inflict considerable damage to flower and vegetable gardens. Like deer, they may need to be fenced out of some areas or away from prized plants.

The most common rabbits in and around suburban gardens are the cottontails. Their larger cousins, the hares, frequent more rural settings. The main difference between rabbits and hares is that cottontails give birth to small, blind, naked young. The young of hares are precocious, born with their eyes open, completely furred and ready to run.

Urban settings are not safe environments for rabbits. Dogs, and particularly cats, take a heavy toll on rabbits' young. The best thing the gardener can offer the cottontail is safe shelter. Thick thorny tangles and blackberry briar patches offer safe haven. Because rabbits and briar patches may not fit one's idea of good gardening, a place for cottontails may not suit many gardens.

Artificial Burrow for Rabbits and Hares

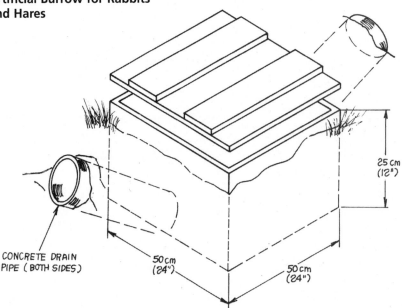

CONCRETE DRAIN PIPE (BOTH SIDES)

50 cm (24")

50 cm (24")

25 cm (12")

Deer Mice and White-footed Mice

Habitat: All manner of habitats with suitable cover.

These native mice, with big ears, large eyes and long tails, delight in scampering about quiet locations such as attics, woodsheds or garages. They occasionally enter houses, but this environment is generally the domain of the introduced house mouse. Though deer and white-footed mice are our most numerous native mice, they become active just after dusk and are difficult to observe. If you want a good close look, use a live trap baited with a little peanut butter.

Dry hollows in stumps, rock walls or cavities under logs are preferred locations for nest sites and daytime retreats. They often build their bulky nests in bluebird-sized nest boxes that are placed too close to the ground or partially screened by vegetation. Denning boxes for these mice should have a second exit near one of the top rear corners.

Deer and white-footed mice are omnivorous, feeding on a wide variety of seeds, berries and animal matter.

Shrews and voles, the latter often called meadow mice, are also common native species. Shrews are largely insectivores that feed almost continuously. Voles are vegetarian. They develop networks of runways and tunnels through meadow and edge vegetation. Both are rather secretive, though they are often active by day.

Chipmunks

Habitat: Adequate cover in the form of stumps, rock and wood piles, thick brush.

Chipmunks are the darlings of the rodent world. Though highly desirable as inhabitants of our gardens, their habit of wandering long distances when gathering food exposes them to many predators, particularly domestic cats. For this reason, their survival is greatly reduced in urban areas.

Gardens with lots of cover, stumps, logs, rock and wood piles combined with thick, fruit-producing shrubbery offer ideal chipmunk habitat. In spring, chipmunks feed on green leaves and shoots until seeds and berries become plentiful. They also eat insects, flowers, fruits, mushrooms and birds' eggs. A feeding platform such as a flat rock, sprinkled with a little bird seed or sunflower seeds, will allow these lovely squirrels to be more easily seen. In the Pacific Northwest chipmunks have a particular liking for saskatoon berries (*Amelanchier alnifolia*).

Gray Squirrels and Fox Squirrels

Habitat: Hardwood forests with denning sites and seed-, fruit- and nut-producing trees and shrubs.

Both gray and fox squirrels have expanded their ranges (or have been introduced) and are quite at home in city parks, gardens and along treed boulevards. Like jays and chickadees, squirrels can be persistent hoarders, carrying away more groceries than they can ever eat. Further, their climbing, jumping and evasive abilities make them very difficult to outwit.

Keeping squirrels away from bird feeders can be a considerable challenge. (Sections in Chapter 16 cover squirrel proofing.) One method that may minimize conflicts is to provide squirrel foods at a special location, then squirrel-proof the remaining bird feeders as best you can. In gardens, they can be a nuisance, digging up and eating tubers and buds. Residences are ideal denning places and their gnawing can inflict considerable damage. For these reasons they may not be our favorite garden guests.

Squirrel Nest Box

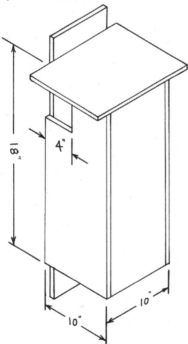

In their defence, they must be admired for their beauty and agility in negotiating urban environments. Their diet is variable, depending on the season. Seed-, nut- and fruit-producing trees take their turn as larders.

Artificial boxes as nesting and denning locations can provide an alternative for squirrels that try to enter your home. These structures in urban environments provide a degree of protection from some predators. This protection has resulted in the proliferation of a number of different color phases, particularly black squirrels.

Where the gray squirrel reaches evergreen forested areas in the Northwest it competes with the Douglas squirrel, with its orange belly, and possibly the white-bellied red squirrel (*Tamiasciurus hudsonicus*). These latter species are more at home in evergreen forests where cones make up a good portion of their diet. All three species can be attracted to gardens stocked with foods such as peanuts or peanut hearts. If nothing else is available, cereal grains will be targeted.

Flying Squirrels

Habitat: Forest sites with cavities for day-time sleeping.

This squirrel, with its beautiful large eyes, is another favorite of the squirrel family, though it is a very fortunate person who has ever seen one. Our species, northern and southern, are nocturnal animals that prefer coniferous forest with a mixture of hardwoods and shrubs. Often they are the most numerous squirrel in an area but because they are so secretive and silent, they are seldom

Northern flying squirrel feeding on sunflower seeds.

seen, even by naturalists. These animals have a membrane that stretches from wrist to ankle, which allows them to make long gliding leaps. Their flattened tails also enhance the gliding process.

Unlike other squirrels, they are social. Several may feed and den together. Though not true hibernators, they remain inactive for prolonged periods during severe winter weather. They cache hordes of nuts and cones as a winter food supply. Gardens that back onto a park or forest are most likely to attract flying squirrels.

In urban and garden settings, they will readily take over a nest box of swallow or bluebird size if it is placed well off the ground (10+ feet or 3 meters) preferably in a coniferous tree. Gnaw marks around the entrance often indicate that a flying squirrel is in residence. Flying squirrels readily visit bird feeders, and a bracket on the side of a tree, baited with sunflower seeds, also attracts them. A nearby artificial light source will enhance the viewing opportunity.

Coyotes

Habitat: Adequate space to den and raise young.

In many urban settings coyotes (and foxes) have become regular visitors. They are large enough and smart enough to turn the tables on would-be predators such as domestic dogs and cats, and they are cunning enough to avoid many of the pitfalls of living alongside city-dwelling humans.

In garden settings these animals will only be transients passing through as they follow their appointed rounds. It is probably unwise to encourage their presence or offer them food. Nonetheless they are magnificent animals that provoke our curiosity.

Raccoons

Habitat: Daytime places to hide; access to ponds and water courses.

The "Lone Ranger" mask of the raccoon makes this animal of the twilight an intriguing backyard guest. They have adapted well to our suburbs, particularly to the way we handle our garbage. In our gardens they can be both a joy and a nuisance. Raccoons find shallow pools or ponds appealing, often giving the plants and animals a good thrashing. Fish, frogs, crayfish and freshwater mussels are a favored part of a raccoon's diet. Raccoons also like to wash their food. In many European languages, the name for raccoon, when translated, means "washing bear." A birdbath by day can become a raccoon's wash basin by night.

A raccoon's diet varies considerably with the season. In the presence of garbage or a well-stocked feeding table, these preferences and patterns disappear. Once habituated to a feeding station, raccoons will appear regularly. Dry dog food has been used with success, but a raw hen's egg is a special treat. It's fun to observe a raccoon's dexterity as it manipulates an egg.

Raccoons are inquisitive mammals that often prowl gardens under cover of darkness.

The Natural Diet of Raccoons by Season

Spring   Predominantly animal matter. Large pond animals; crayfish, clams, frogs, water beetles, etc.
Young animals, birds and eggs.

Summer   About 70% vegetarian. Berries, seeds and fruits; vegetables, particularly corn.
About 30% animal matter. Pond life, frogs, insects, crayfish, etc.

Autumn   Predominantly vegetarian. Fruits, nuts and corn. Bee, termite and ant larvae.

Winter   Mostly animal matter. Animal carcasses, stored body fat.

Raccoons have a number of negative qualities that should concern the wildlife gardener. One is that they are serious predators of smaller animals and delight in raiding bird nests. When raccoons are known to be around, protect bird nesting locations.

Raccoons, like other nocturnal animals, require a quiet, safe daytime hideaway. This can be an attic, a culvert, vacant building or other suitable retreat. In natural settings these sites are often large hollow logs or trees, dense tangles of vegetation or even an old crow's nest. Providing a daytime den for raccoons is not without risk of incurring property damage or the potential of a transmittable disease. However, if this den is placed well away from a residence, the risks are greatly reduced.

Diseases such as distemper (both canine and feline) and rabies are known to affect raccoons. For this reason any animal that appears disoriented or is encountered under unnatural situations must be considered suspect. *Never touch, pet or try to handle these animals.*

Striped Skunks

Habitat: Places to build underground burrows with nearby sources of fruit, insects and small mammals.

Like raccoons and coyotes, skunks have also moved into urban neighborhoods. Today it is not uncommon to get a waft of "eau du skunk" in many unexpected places. Skunks, like all members of the weasel family, have prominent anal scent glands. The skunk branch of the family has taken this feature to the extreme, and secretions from these glands have become a potent defense mechanism.

In the northern parts of their range, skunks are true hibernators, building or taking over a burrow which they line with available grasses and leaves. In the south they become dormant only during cold spells. Sometimes a number of individuals hibernate or den together.

Like raccoons, a skunk's diet varies according to the season. Skunks can be conditioned to the offerings of a feeding table, but most homeowners will not likely want to encourage these visitors. Small amounts of food will keep these animals coming back; too much food may bring an army of visitors and encourage scrapping and bickering with each other and with raccoons that may leave a nasty fragrance in your garden. If you do have a skunk feeding station, keep it well away from your house.

Little Brown Bats

Habitat: Daytime hideaway with a nearby pond or water course.

Of the many species of bats, the most commonly encountered species around our homes and gardens are the little brown bats. They are often seen at twilight as they emerge from their daytime roosts. Often their first foray is to a neighboring pond for a drink. The big brown bat (*Eptesicus fuscus*) is also a common bat of suburban areas. Often it occurs in association with its smaller relatives.

Bats eat a prodigious number of insects in relation to their body weight, primarily moths, beetles, bugs and soft-bodied flying insects. The bat traps insects by bringing the tail membrane forward under the body. Insects are either eaten on the wing or are taken to a perch. Although bats do eat mosquitoes, they most often feed on larger prey, such as moths, mayflies, caddisflies and even beetles.

In natural situations bats roost under bark, in hollow trees and in caves. In urban settings they use attics, church steeples, hollow walls and other similar dark, quiet places with an appropriate entrance. Even a rough split shake roof is a good hide-away for bats. A large opening is not required for them to gain access. Bats have been known to enter through a space no larger than a dime!

Efforts in recent years to provide artificial bat houses in gardens have

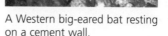

A Western big-eared bat resting on a cement wall.

proved disappointing. Perhaps the answer lies in building bat houses into our homes as "false fronts." A primary concern must be that the remainder of your home is sealed off and secure so that bats cannot get into attics and walls, where they could cause damage.

Some bats, like birds, migrate relatively long distances in spring and fall. Every once in a while, when these migrations are taking place, bats can be found clinging to the sides of buildings, often those with rough concrete walls. Here they may rest for a few days. Anytime bats are found in these situations, it is wise not to handle them. Very few bats have been found to carry rabies, but rabies and other diseases are a possibility. If handling is necessary, always wear sturdy gloves or pick bats up with a shovel or dust pan. Public health officials may be interested in testing these animals.

When inspecting attics and crawl spaces where bats may be roosting, play it safe. The bats themselves are not dangerous, but inhaling guano or dust from bat roosts can be lethal. *Always wear a respirator mask.*

Enhancing Gardens for Small Mammals

A few simple guidelines will allow you to appreciate and enjoy the presence of small mammals in your garden without putting other animals, your house or yourself at risk. Place your mammal feeding station a reasonable distance from your home but in a location that provides a good unhindered view. As different mammals have different food tastes, more than one feeding station may be desirable. It is often best to keep species separated, particularly when mothers and their young are still traveling together.

Install a garden lighting system so you can more easily view nocturnal species. An elevated light source will allow better viewing of the nocturnal animals that visit your garden. The light also attracts insects that will provide a supplemental food source to many species.

Elevated feeding platforms, such as a tree stump or flat-topped rock, are ideal. Put out only a little food each time—just enough to keep them coming back but not enough to keep them hanging around all the time. This will allow you to see them regularly, but you will not be inundated or see your garden damaged. Those that come first are the first served.

Planting nut-, berry-, fruit- and seed-producing plants, especially trees and shrubs, around the periphery of your garden will attract many of these species. Where fruit becomes an issue (that is, who gets the fruit, gardener or wildlife), a compromise may be required. A metal or stiff plastic collar around the trunk may prevent animals from climbing into the tree but allows them to enjoy fallen fruit on the ground.

The need for water can be met with a small pool or an easily accessible birdbath. To keep the water in the birdbath fresh, a dripping system (see Chapter 10), with a scrubbing-out once in a while is recommended.

CHAPTER 8
Gardening for Hummingbirds

Our smallest birds, hummingbirds are tiny bundles of energy that are both beautiful and fascinating to watch. This totally American family of 300+ species has its center of distribution in South and Central America. Eight species stretch north into the area covered by this guide. Another 10 just venture into Arizona and/or Texas and two Caribbean species wander to southern Florida. Of our eight common species, one, the rufous hummingbird, gets as far north as Anchorage, Alaska.

These birds are the counterparts of the sunbirds of Asia and Africa and the honeyeaters of Australia. All three groups are nectar feeders, getting a goodly part of their diet from nectar-producing flowers. While many of the honeyeaters are somewhat drab, the sunbirds and hummers often glisten. The male hummingbird's throat hackles, or gorget, reflect iridescent sheens that sparkle as they catch the light. Another distinctive feature of hummingbirds is the long rapier-like bill of many species, used for probing tubular flowers. Within the bill is an equally remarkably tongue, even longer than the bill, for collecting nectar. The tip of this bill is pliable and very sensitive.

Not all hummingbirds are long-billed. Some are adapted to other food sources and have short or curved bills. During courtship and when feeding, bills can become weapons.

A hummingbird's particular anatomy and physiology and its ability to individually control its flight feathers allow it to hover with ease, fly backwards and perform maneuvers no other bird can accomplish. With a heart rate sometimes exceeding 1,200 beats per minute, you might think hummingbirds would burn out quickly, but that's far from the truth. The average longevity of hummingbirds is thought to be longer than sparrows', maybe even longer than robins'.

The Anna's hummingbird remains in the Pacific Northwest all winter. Even when the ground is covered with snow, they visit feeders that have frozen solid! In these conditions, people bring their feeders inside at night and place them out again in the morning, replacing them as required during the day, to ensure the sugar-water mix is continually available. While feeders are helpful, the Anna's major dietary item during the winter months is small flying insects. The Anna's hummingbird can remain in the northwest because, like a number of other birds and mammals, it has developed the ability to lower its body temperature to enter a torpid state. This saves energy, allowing birds to survive long cold nights and spells of inclement weather.

Anna's hummingbird aside, most of our hummingbird species migrate considerable distances. The ruby-throat migrates across the Caribbean as far south as Panama, the rufous hummer winters from Mexico south. These are long migrations for such a small bird. When the first nectar-bearing flowers appear in spring, these birds return northward.

The presence of a variety of hummingbird flowers, primarily those that are red or orange and tubular in design (see "Some Native Plants Attractive to Hummingbirds", page 75) are certain to attract local hummingbirds into your garden. Select flower species that provide an overlap in blooming periods. Hummingbird feeders also help. Be sure the mixture remains fresh by replacing it every two days, and give the container a good cleaning between fillings.

Concern has been expressed that hummingbird feeders may be detrimental to hummingbird populations on a number

House Finches at Hummingbird Feeders

House finches and orioles and a number of other bird species are sometimes also attracted to the solution in hummingbird feeders. These non-hovering species can be allowed access to your nectar feeder by adding a couple of perches (see photo). If you want to discourage these species, simply remove the perches. If house finches or orioles become numerous, sugar water can be dispensed from a water bottle.

of grounds. One is addiction, the fear being that hummingbirds, in the presence of feeders, will not migrate normally. This is not the case, as hummingbirds move away from feeders, often to flower meadows at higher elevation, well before they begin their migration, even where flower nectar is readily available. Along the west coast, the migration of rufous hummers follows the coast and valleys north in spring and the mountain meadows south in fall, taking advantage of the earliest and latest flower blooming.

A number of bird species have been studied, and it has been found that even in the presence of feeding stations wild birds still spend a considerable time foraging naturally. In my own garden, where Anna's hummingbirds are present year round, you might think that feeding activity around a sugar-water feeder would be most intense during the winter. This has been observed not to be the case.

A second fear is that feeders provide hummingbirds with an inappropriate diet. There is no information to support this contention, though it is recommended that the mixture be strictly white granulated sugar and pure water. No color additives or supplements are needed or recommended. (See page 77 for details of feeders).

Paper Birch, Sapsuckers and Hummingbirds

These three organisms might appear to be an unusual combination, but they do form an association of sorts. Birch trees produce a high-quality sap, favored and worked by the woodpeckers we know as sapsuckers. Hummingbirds, bees, ants and even smaller insects steal the sap when the developer is absent. Around sap wells, the interaction of these species can be fascinating to watch, as sapsucker, hummingbirds and bees vie with one another.

While the gardener cannot be guaranteed that his or her birch tree will become a sapsucker tree, having a white or paper birch as part of the garden landscape opens the door should a sapsucker take up residence in your neighborhood.

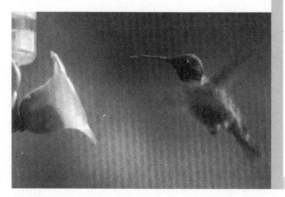

Common North American Hummingbirds

Hummingbird	Description	Where Found
Ruby-throated	Green and white, male with ruby-red gorget.	Central and eastern states, southern Canada, including the prairie provinces where it is likely the only species present.
Black-chinned	Green and white, male has two-toned black and violet gorget.	Semi-arid lands of western states from southern British Columbia south.
Costa's	Smallish green and white hummer, male with deep violet crown and gorget.	Southern California and Arizona.
Anna's	Robust green and gray male with magenta crown and gorget.	Along Pacific Coast to southern British Columbia, eastern Vancouver Island.
Calliope	Small green and white, male gorget a series of purple-red slashes. Female with rusty flanks.	Mountain country and canyons of far west, central British Columbia southward.
Broad-tailed	Green and white, male with red gorget. Female with rusty flanks.	Rocky Mountain; Great Basin area.
Rufous	Rufous brown and green, male gorget ruby-red.	Northwest states, British Columbia, south coastal Alaska.
Allen's	Similar to rufous but male has green back. Female and immatures indistinguishable from rufous.	Coastal California.

Consult a bird field guide for further information on identifying these species. Females and immature birds are often very difficult to identify with certainty.

Choosing the Best Plants

A huge variety of flowering plants suitable to a hummingbird garden is available. While local nurseries may not stock many native plants, they can advise where they might be obtained.

Much research, genetic selection and manipulation has taken place in the horticultural world, but few researchers have thought about hummingbirds during this development. More likely it has been the color and form of the flowers or foliage. As a result, the value to hummingbirds of the original plants may well have been diminished. Ask for recommendations and then observe what plants do best in your garden. The following charts will give you a starting point. Also see page 79 for using some plants to create a tower of flowers.

Some Native Plants Attractive to Hummingbirds	Blooming Times/ Comments
Shrubs	
Red-flowering currant (*Ribes sanguineum*)	Early spring, west coast.
Salmonberry (*Rubus spectabilis*)	Early spring, west coast.
Penstemons (*Penstemon* species)	Late spring and summer.
Vines and Climbers	
Orange honeysuckle (*Lonicera ciliosa*)	Mid to late spring.
Trumpet creeper (*Campsis radicans*)	Summer. Native to northeast, fast-growing.
Flowers	
Columbine (*Aquilegia* species)	Midspring through summer.
Bee balm (*Monarda* species)	Summer.
Scarlet gilia (*Ipomopsis aggregata*)	Summer. Western dry areas.
Hedge nettle (*Stachys* species)	Summer. Moist shaded areas.
Fireweed (*Epilobium angustifolium*)	Late spring and summer. Could be invasive.
Cardinal flower (*Lobelia cardinalis*)	Summer. Likes moist soils.
Touch-me-not (*Impatiens* species)	Summer. A variety of species; has exploding seed pods!
Ocotillo (*Fouquieria splendens*)	Desert areas of southwest.

Introduced Plants Attractive to Hummingbirds	Blooming Times/ Comments
Trees	
Horsechestnut (*Aesculus* species)	Summer. Pink or red forms best.
Locust (*Robinia* species)	Summer. Fast growing, often suckers.
Catalpa (*Catalpa speciosa*)	Summer. Hardy and deciduous.
Shrubs	
Butterfly bush (*Buddleia davidii*)	Summer. Hardy and colorful.
Lilac (*Syringa* species)	Late spring. Many varieties.
Siberian pea (*Caragana arborescens*)	Summer. Hardy, fast-growing, sweet-scented flowers.
Weigela (*Weigela* species)	Summer. Many varieties.
Flowering quince (*Chaenomeles* species)	Spring. Many varieties and flower colors.
Vines and Climbers	
Scarlet runner bean (*Phaseolus coccineus*)	Summer. Enjoy the beans after the hummingbirds have pollinated the flowers.
Honeysuckle (*Lonicera* species)	Many varieties and colors.
Nasturtium (*Tropaeolum majus*)	Easy to grow as an annual in moist soils; many colors available.
Flowers	
Fuchsia (*Fuschia* species)	Late spring and summer. Single flowers best, good in hanging baskets.
Red-hot poker (*Kniphofia uvaria*)	Early summer. Heat and drought tolerant.
Montbretia (*Crocosmia crocosmiiflora*)	Showy orange flowers in summer.
Petunia (*Petunia* species)	Provides splashes of color over a long blooming period.
Larkspur (*Delphinium* species)	Summer. Red-flowered species best.
Sage (*Salvia* species)	Many color forms to choose from.

Using a Hummingbird Feeder

Much has been written about what should and should not be included in hummingbird feeding solutions. Research on natural nectars produced by plants indicates the syrup that flowers produce is relatively weak. This should not be surprising, as flowers that depend on birds for pollination need the birds to return as often as possible. An abundant but low sugar content solution will keep the birds coming back, giving a better chance of pollination.

Hummingbirds can be quite discerning. One study at Victoria, B.C., tested the attractiveness of solutions varying from 5% to 75% on Anna's hummingbirds. (A 5% solution would be 5 mL of sugar to 100 mL water.) The birds favored the strongest solution available. Nonetheless, the recommendation here is to supply a solution of one part white granulated sugar to three or four parts boiling water (see below). This is probably ideal, as it approximates the natural sugar content of hummingbird flower nectar.

While red is a well-known attractant to hummingbirds, the addition of red food coloring to the sugar water solution in feeders does little to improve the end result. As long as the feeder has a red lure when it is first placed outside each season, this should suffice. Once a hummingbird finds the solution, a lure almost becomes unnecessary.

Fermentation and Molds

Natural yeast and molds are everywhere, and it is quite possible that they will begin the fermentation process inside your feeder without you ever being aware of it. This happens more quickly during hot weather or in the presence of additives to the basic sugar-water recipe.

To reduce the chances of spoiling, wash your feeder thoroughly between each filling. When the weather is hot, replace the unused solution every second day. Here is a helpful suggestion: use two feeders on a shuttle basis, taking the fresh one out when you bring the old solution in. Use

Honey

Honey in its commercial forms is dangerous to hummingbirds as it may cause fungal growths on their tongues or throats. The only safe honey is honey straight from the hive, but the best precaution is not to use honey at all.

boiling water to make the sugar water; this will kill most of the yeast and mold spores. Once the solution cools, it is ready for use. Surplus solution can be stored in the refrigerator.

Locating Your Feeder

Selecting the best place for a feeder requires a little thought. To allow the hummingbirds to find the feeder in the first place, it should be placed out in the open. Once they get used to coming, it can be relocated, by increments, somewhere more visible to you or a place that provides shelter or protection.

Hummingbirds enjoy perching near a feeding source, where they keep a wary eye open for competitors and other hummers who would usurp their syrup. The shenanigans around a feeder can become bizarre. Nearby trees with a few small, fine, dead branches make ideal perches, as hummingbirds have tiny feet.

All feeders should be placed well off the ground, at least 6½ feet (2 m), out of reach of ground-frequenting predators, particularly cats. Where this height is not available, place a 24-inch (60-cm) circle of chicken wire or lathing screen loosely below the feeder. This will act as an effective barrier to leaping cats.

Controlling Wasps, Bees and Ants

Sugar is a well-known food of the honey bee, so it should not be surprising that its cousins, wasps and hornets, also have a liking for this mixture. If given a free reign, they will drive hummingbirds from the feeder, not to mention consume large quantities of syrup. Many suppliers have developed bee guards for hummingbird feeders that screen these pests out. As soon as they realize they cannot get at the solution, they will abandon their quest. (Chapter 16 provides some additional ideas for wasp and hornet control.)

Ants, particularly the smaller species, are more difficult to discourage. I have had some success using fine monofilament fishing leader (3-pound test) to suspend the feeder. Most ants have difficulty climbing down a short single strand of this nylon. Commercially available sticky products that tangle the feet can also be successful.

Hummingbird Nesting Material Dispenser

Hummingbird feeders are the easiest way to attract hummers to your garden, but you might want to try the following. Visit your local cattail marsh and bring home two heads with good long stems. Place these in your garden in plain view, as high above the ground as possible—6½ feet (2 m) at a minimum—and watch what happens as birds begin nesting. Female hummingbirds find cattail down an ideal nesting material. They return repeatedly for beakfuls of fluff, which they knead into their nests. Only the female undertakes nest building, incubation and chick rearing.

Trying to follow a female to her nest is a challenge. She simply "rockets" away, making it impossible to follow.

Gorget Iridescence

The brilliance of the male hummingbird's iridescence is created by minute prisms within each feather that reflect light. The color varies on how light strikes the feather and the angle at which it is viewed. The structure of these prisms is unique to each species, accounting for the different colors.

Some years ago a friend watched a hummingbird bounce off a window. While it lay stunned on the ground for a few moments, a photo was taken. The bird in the photo was tentatively identified as a male Costa's hummingbird, but this seemed impossible to confirm.

An inspection of the window revealed two tiny feathers stuck to the pane. Close examination revealed them to be gorget feathers. Their iridescence matched those of the Costa's. These two feathers are the only specimen documentation of the Costa's hummingbird for British Columbia and, in fact, all of Canada.

Tower of flowers

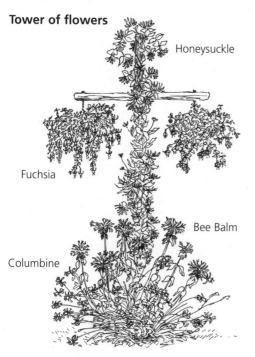

Honeysuckle

Fuchsia

Bee Balm

Columbine

Courtship Display—Anna's Hummingbird

Male hummingbirds are the first to arrive in spring, closely followed by the females. Then the courtship fun begins. Each species has its own particular display, and some are quite elaborate. The Anna's is said to be one of the few "singing" hummingbirds, but all species are able to produce some sound in addition to the whir or hum of their wings.

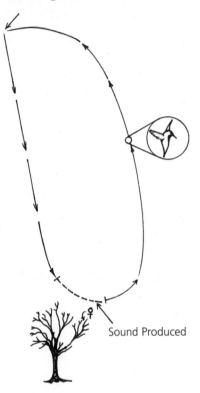

Display Flight of Anna's Hummingbird

Sound Produced

From a prominent perch the male Anna's utters a series of distinct rasping buzzes. When another small bird, rival male or a female appears, it zooms high overhead, then power-dives at the object of its attention, uttering a loud *ee-a-k* as it passes nearby. This may be repeated several times in quick succession. The display of the ruby-throated, rather than following the Anna's ellipse, moves back and forth, like a pendulum.

A Mist Bather for Hummingbirds

Hummingbirds seldom land, robin-fashion, to take a bath. They have been observed clinging to water-saturated, mossy, vertical surfaces and splashing themselves. More often they fly through or hover in fine sprays from garden sprinklers. Fine sprayers have been developed to provide small birds, particularly hummingbirds, bathing opportunities. These are available from specialty stores.

CHAPTER 9
Gardening for Spring Birds

Without question, songbirds are the most popular and desirable of all backyard wildlife. To encourage and ensure their presence, we spend millions of dollars annually catering to their needs. These generally small, hyperactive birds spend almost their entire lives (when not roosting) in their quest for food. This gives gardeners the opportunity and challenge of improving their garden settings for these colorful and by no means quiet songsters.

As the seasons change, the general attractiveness of our gardens to urban birds also changes. As this happens, the backyard manager must modify his or her strategies and change tactics. The axiom for attracting birds is simply to supply what the birds need most. With some exceptions, these are nesting sites in spring, water in summer and food and shelter in winter. Because there is so much interest in birds, and so much information available, in this book each season is afforded its own chapter.

Spring is the season for new arrivals. As the days lengthen and the ambient temperatures increase, common garden birds begin their migrations. In northern areas this may begin as early as February with the arrival of the common crow and red-winged blackbirds. Following close behind are the true harbingers of spring—the violet-green and tree swallows. With the arrival of each new wave, others depart, as the dynamic phenomena of migration plays itself out. The parade culminates with the arrival or passage of the common nighthawk, in May or early June.

With the departure of winter snows and the greening of the countryside, supplemental feeding from bird feeders assumes less importance. As natural foods become more readily available, many people phase out their winter feeding stations. You may want to scale down rather than discontinue this practice, as a few resident birds may still be regular guests. A few good mulchings of the ground below feeders will deter unwanted weed and seed germination.

For birders, as bird watchers are known, spring is an exciting season. Depending on weather patterns and cloud cover, many unusual birds might arrive in your garden. A good bird book, one of the popular field guides, and a pair of binoculars are musts if you wish to know who's who. Simply watching and recording the birds passing through during this season is a meaningful challenge.

As the migration subsides, the breeding season commences. For your backyard residents, the ritual and preparation for this becomes a preoccupation, especially for the males of each species. The gardener who knows nesting site preferences can also focus his or her activities in anticipation of this event.

Birdhouses and nesting brackets are two ways of ensuring some species will nest on your property. Providing appropriate nesting habitat, thick shrubbery or a dead snag for those species that do not nest in boxes is a second consideration. A third is providing appropriate nesting materials. Offering diverse nest box sizes and shapes, nesting habitats and nesting materials will enrich the variety of birds present in the spring garden.

Birdhouses for the Nest Box Nesters

Nesting structures are easily built from almost any type of material, including ceramics, metal, plastic and even cardboard. Wood is the most readily available and is preferred because of its natural properties.

Nesting structures may be built in all manner of shapes and sizes. The one illustrated here (see page 85) is simple to make and in my experience has produced good results. Over the years efforts have been made to tailor these structures to the special needs of individual species. This is especially true for bluebirds. Each species (see chart, next page) has its own preferences as to size, shape, hole size and height at which the boxes are placed above the ground. Robins and barn swallows require only a simple shelf or bracket (detailed on page 87).

Generally speaking, the simpler and more natural a nest box is, both in shape and materials, the better its chances of being used.

Paints and stains are not necessary. In fact they may even be detrimental.

Keeping things simple is an axiom worth remembering when it comes to birdhouse construction. Recycling old building or fence materials and using these for birdhouses will impart a more natural, weathered look. If you have the patience, you can age freshly cut boards, such as cedar, by leaving them outside exposed to the elements over winter.

Having said that paint is unnecessary, or even detrimental, it is interesting to note that boxes painted white inside have higher occupancy rates than those painted black inside. If you want to paint your nest boxes, do this early in the fall season so paint vapors will be gone by spring. While most birds do not have a sense of smell, this will give the box a little time to season.

Some cavity nesters, like woodpeckers and chickadees, will use nest boxes. A few wood chips or a handful of coarse sawdust in the bottom will add to their naturalness.

Nest Box Measurements for Common Garden Birds

Swallows The hole size should be 1½ x 1½ inches (2.5 x 4 cm) and placed 4 inches (10 cm) from the floor and 5 inches (12 cm) from the roof. The floor area should be 5 x 5 inches (13 x 13 cm) and the box should be 10–17 feet (3–5 m) above the ground.

Chickadees The hole size should be 1⅕ (3 cm) and placed 6 inches (15 cm) from the floor and 5 inches (12 cm) from the roof. The floor area should be 3½ x 3½ inches (9 x 9 cm) and the box should be 6½–17 feet (2–5 m) above the ground.

Wrens The hole size should be 1½ x 1½ inches (2.5 x 4 cm) and placed 4 inches (10 cm) from the floor and 5 inches (12 cm) from the roof. The floor area should be 5 x 5 inches (13 x 13 cm) and the box should be 10–17 feet (3–5 m) above the ground.

Bluebirds The hole size should be 1½ x 1½ inches (2.5 x 4 cm) and placed 4 inches (10 cm) from the floor and 5 inches (12 cm) from the roof. The floor area should be 5 x 5 inches (13 x 13 cm) and the box should be 10–17 feet (3–5 m) above the ground.

Nest Boxes for Purple Martins

The area east of the Rocky Mountains and along the west coast of the continent as far north as Vancouver Island is the purple martin nesting range. Our largest swallow, this graceful bird has inspired more birdhouse architecture than possibly any other, worldwide. Native North Americans encouraged their nesting in gourds, and these fruits, properly cleaned out and prepared, are still good nesting sites.

Martins prefer to nest in groups, and this has encouraged wildlife enthusiasts to erect multiple compartment houses that can be used by a number of breeding pairs. The general specifications are a 2-inch (5-cm) entrance hole, placed fairly close to the floor of a 6-inch x 8-inch (15- x 20-cm) compartment. From this starting point, the possibilities are virtually endless in size, form and degree of elaboration. Boxes should be placed at least 16 feet (5 m) above the ground.

Martin houses are the ideal dimensions for starlings and house sparrows, and this can be a problem, as these birds are very bossy and territorial around their nesting locations. You can make the hole ½ inch (1.2 cm) larger and oval in shape, but the best plan is to take the nest box down for the winter and not put it up again until just after the first purple martins return in the spring. (See "Discouraging House Sparrows and Starlings," next page.)

Hole Sizes and Shapes to Deter House Sparrows

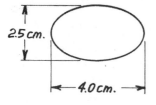

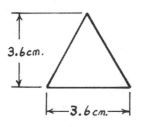

Nest Boxes for House Sparrows and Starlings

To wildlife watchers, house sparrows and European starlings are controversial birds. Despised they may be by some, but their presence can bring considerable joy in areas where few native birds may be found. Both build large, untidy, bulky nests. Nest boxes require a fairly large entrance: 1½ inches (4 cm) for house sparrows and 2 to 2½ inches (5 to 6 cm) for starlings. The other box measurements for house sparrows should equal those given for bluebirds, and, in the case of starlings, be larger than those given for bluebirds (page 83).

A Simple Nest Box Design

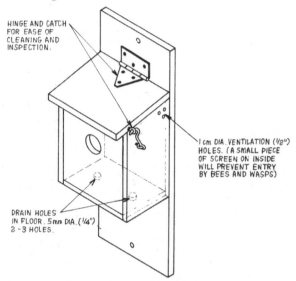

HINGE AND CATCH FOR EASE OF CLEANING AND INSPECTION.

1 cm DIA. VENTILATION (½") HOLES. (A SMALL PIECE OF SCREEN ON INSIDE WILL PREVENT ENTRY BY BEES AND WASPS)

DRAIN HOLES IN FLOOR. 5mm DIA. (¼") 2-3 HOLES.

Discouraging House Sparrows and Starlings

Here are a number of suggestions to discourage starlings and house sparrows from using boxes intended for other birds.

- Make the hole oval or triangular. This allows swallows to enter but keeps house sparrows at bay.

- Keep the boxes small and deep for chickadees, or move the hole 1⅕ inches (3 cm) closer to the floor for swallows.

- Wait until you see the species you want, such as swallows, inspecting for nesting locations, then put up your nest box.

- Place boxes where you can scare away unwanted nesters.

- Locate nest boxes for chickadees and wrens in partially secluded locations screened by deciduous vegetation (wrens) and evergreens (chickadees).

- For swallows, increase the thickness of the front panel to make it at least 1½ inches (4 cm) deep.

Nest Platforms for Robins and Barn Swallows

Robins and barn swallows are partial to nesting under the eaves of houses where a suitable platform exists. For robins, a platform at least 6 x 6 inches (15 x 15 cm) with a slight lip placed 8 to 10 inches (20 to 25 cm) below the soffit should give good results. A little greenery, in the form of plastic foliage placed around the lip, improves results.

For barn swallows, a 4-inch (10-cm) block of 2 x 3 nailed 6 inches (15 cm) below the soffit will provide enough nesting support for their mud nests. Rough wood is best as mud sticks to it more readily.

Annual Maintenance

At the beginning of spring, before the potential species start showing an interest in nest building, the old nests from previous seasons should be removed and the boxes given a good cleaning. In addition to removing the accumulated dirt, this will also remove any parasites, making the box more hygienic.

The reason behind this annual maintenance program, specifically the removal of potential parasites, is not as simple as it might seem. Parasites have parasites too!

One of the common parasites, particularly of young barn swallows, is a species of blowfly whose maggots suck blood from the nestling birds. Once these larvae pupate, they in turn become the prey of a number of wasp species. This complex relationship of birds to blowflies to wasps has evolved over eons.

When positioning the box, understand the preferences of the bird for which the house was selected. For instance, swallows and bluebirds nest in areas with a clear, open approach. Chickadees and wrens appreciate a little seclusion or nearby vegetation.

Avoid exposure to full sun, prevailing winds and driving or heavy rains. Easterly or westerly exposures for the entrance are best.

If you are putting up a number of boxes, space them well apart and/or have them face in different directions. This lessens competition. The average garden can accommodate three or four boxes at most, each usually designed for a different species.

Avoid areas where predators, especially cats, are present or areas that give easy access to predators such as squirrels or snakes.

Robin Shelf and Barn Swallow Bracket

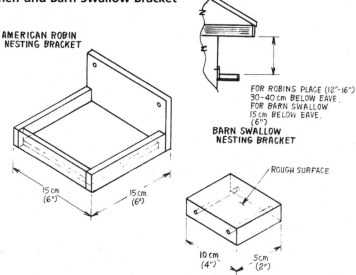

AMERICAN ROBIN
NESTING BRACKET

FOR ROBINS PLACE (12"-16")
30-40 cm BELOW EAVE
FOR BARN SWALLOW
15 cm BELOW EAVE.
(6")

BARN SWALLOW
NESTING BRACKET

ROUGH SURFACE

15 cm
(6")

15 cm
(6")

10 cm
(4")

5 cm
(2")

When it comes to birdhouse maintenance, cleaning with disin-
fectants disrupts this natural balance. While there are many interesting and practical arguments on both sides of the question of
intervening in such a natural chain, the important thing to remember is that we still have barn swallows where they nest naturally
and are exposed to parasites.

Nest boxes are not natural cavities. Generally when we compare
natural cavity sizes to those recommended for birdhouses, the natural ones are smaller, more compact and require less nesting material. Therefore there might be less space for potential parasites.

From this, perhaps there are two lessons to be learned. First, we
should make our birdhouses a little smaller, so that the nesting
space more closely approximates those of natural cavities, and second, the simple removal of old nesting materials each spring
should be the extent of our annual maintenance program.

The "Do It Themselves" Species

Woodpeckers, nuthatches and chickadees often prefer to build
their own nesting chambers in dead trees or snags. Snags for nesting purposes can be either created or imported. You can create a
snag by girdling a live tree and waiting, but it takes a long time for
the wood to reach the appropriate softness for these species to

excavate easily. Hardwoods such as maple, and birch are the best trees for this purpose as they deteriorate faster than softwoods.

When creating a snag, choose a downed log that is already partially decayed, if possible. Logs should be 10 to 17 ft. (3 to 5 m) in length and 6 to 12 inches (15 to 30 cm) in diameter. To hasten the softening process, when using a fresh log, place it on moist ground and cover it with leaf litter. One or two years of this treatment should soften the wood to the desired state.

Bird Territories

The term *territory* is generally considered to be a defended area, occupied by an individual, a pair or a group of birds. While this definition appears quite simple, there are many types of territories documented that cover many and different aspects of a species' lifestyle.

For songbirds, spring is the time when this concept becomes significant in our gardens. At this time males attempt to stake out their territories through song. They also endeavor to physically keep rivals at bay. Their ability to hold a particular piece of real estate (and attract a mate) will help determine how many offspring they will contribute to their population. The general effect (advantage) of territoriality is to spread the individuals of a species out over the available land.

Tree- and Shrub-Nesting Species

Providing nest sites for the tree- and shrub-nesting species is not as easy as making preparations for the nest box crowd. Often it takes a number of years for a tree or shrub to reach the desired size or form. Even when it reaches this size, it is the bird's choice when it comes to choosing which tree or shrub to nest in. The following chart contains some information on the nesting particulars for a few common garden nesting species. These often vary from south to north and east to west.

With the exception of the dark-eyed junco, which nests on the ground, many of the more common garden birds show a preference for fairly mature evergreen or orchard tree species, such as apple. To some degree, all trees and shrubs can be improved as nesting habitat through careful pruning. The aim should be to provide clumps of thicker or denser foliage against trunks or along branches.

In the average garden, house finches are perhaps the most common of the nesting birds, showing a preference for ornamental evergreen shrubs. In eastern

North America these birds often use nest boxes, but seldom do so in the west. Whatever the kind of bird, a dash of luck is still required when encouraging them to nest in your garden.

Some Common Garden Birds

Species	Nest Height	Preferred Location
Eastern phoebe	6½–17 feet (2–5 m)	On beam or rafter under bridges or inside buildings, such as sheds and garages, with easy access from the outside. Note: In the west, Say's phoebe often nests in similar locations.
Blue jay	6½–20 feet (2–6 m)	Well hidden in dense foliage of evergreen trees.
Cedar waxwing	6½–20 feet (2–6 m)	Concealed in thick vegetation of a wide variety of native and ornamental evergreen and deciduous trees and shrubs.
Northern oriole	17–35 feet (5–10 m)	Beautiful hanging nests generally suspended high up in deciduous trees.
Dark-eyed junco	on the ground	Usually near the top of a steep bank where the soil pulls away from the roots of the vegetation above.
Northern cardinal	3–8 feet (1–2.5 m)	In thickets and tangles of dense shrubbery.
House finch	5–15 feet (1.5–4.5 m)	Secluded in native or ornamental evergreen trees, orchard trees. Occasionally in hanging baskets, on ivy-covered walls or in birdhouses.
Chipping sparrow	3–10 feet (1–3 m)	Nestled into thick "knots" of lateral branches of native evergreens or orchard trees.
Song sparrow	near the ground	In dense grass or shrub tangles, often in riparian vegetation.

Providing Nesting Materials

At some time or another, just about every conceivable material might find its way into the construction of a bird's nest. While string, straw, feathers and mud are common components, cellophane, shoelaces, snake skins and even dry animal scats are not unknown. Some common household and garden materials used by many of our garden birds are listed in the following chart. This list is not exhaustive. Many birds are quite specific, almost fussy, about the materials they use.

If you have one of the swallow species nesting near your home, you may wish to "feed" them white feathers! About the middle of May, possibly a little earlier in more southerly locations, as nest building is nearing completion, violet-green, tree and barn swallows search out white feathers to line their nests. During this period it can be great fun to drop feathers from an elevated window or porch and watch the swallows catch them as they drift on the breeze. Downy white feathers seem to be favored.

Nesting materials can be dispensed in a number of ways. An onion bag, filled with cattail down or pet combings, is an easy way to hang out these materials. Chickadees have been seen to land on a sleeping dog to gather hair.

Mud is an important nesting material. Where good-quality mud is not easy to come by, a small mud puddle, kept moist with a regular sprinkling of water, will do the trick. Years ago, park naturalists in British Columbia made it an annual practice to import a small bag of mud to a rocky islet where barn swallows had never nested. The swallows began nesting, and in return the naturalists got a small measure of mosquito control. The practice continues to this day.

BBC's— The Breeding Bird Counts

Every spring thousands of bird enthusiasts take to the backroads to census our wild bird populations across the continent. Each predetermined 25-mile (40-km) route has 50 three-minute listening stations. Enumerators record species by song, and when the results of all these counts are compiled and compared on a year-to-year basis, distribution and population trends of each species can be determined.

The bird counts are coordinated by the United States Fish and Wildlife Service and in Canada by the Canadian Wildlife Service.

Preferred Nesting Materials of Some Common Garden Birds

Materials	Users
Straw, grass or weed stems, etc.	
- coarse	Robins, northern cardinal, starlings and house sparrows
- fine	Juncos, sparrows and finches
String (short lengths)	Robins, chickadees and orioles
Moss	Chickadees, phoebes and robins
Lichens	Hummingbirds
Rootlets	Blue jay and siskins
Twigs (large) and cedar bark	Blue jays and crows
Twigs (small)	Northern cardinal and wrens
Hair of domestic animals, deer, etc.	Chipping sparrows, chickadees
Feathers	Swallows in particular
Cotton, kapok, cattail down	Wrens, chickadees and hummingbirds
Mud	Robins, phoebes, barn and cliff swallows

Singing Stations

The bird order is divided into two roughly equal major divisions—the non-passerines and the passerines. We better appreciate and know the passerines as songbirds, on account of their musical vocalizations. These are primarily the birds that frequent our gardens, though a few non-passerines, such as woodpeckers, pigeons and hummingbirds, can be garden birds as well.

As well as giving us visual enjoyment, birds are endlessly fascinating in their vocalizations. Almost without exception, all our garden birds, even hummingbirds and woodpeckers, have their own particular sounds, calls or songs.

During the courtship and pairing process, male songbirds are at their most vocal. To hear this chorus at its best, be prepared to get up early. Depending on your location (earlier in the south and later in the far north), mid-May to early June is the time when the dawn chorus is at its peak. Identifying the species by their songs is an interesting challenge. Once mastered, you can just about throw away your binoculars and bird books and conduct a roll call using only your ears. With a little practice, you will soon be able to identify each bird by its call. For very wide-ranging birds, like the song sparrow, populations in different parts of the country have different dialects. Top-notch birders can identify virtually every kind of bird—more than 650 in North America—just by listening to their call!

Some birds sing from seclusion: others, often the highly colored or brightly marked ones, sing in the open, where they can easily be observed. These viewing opportunities can be enhanced with a little selective pruning or by girdling one or two of the leaders of selected deciduous shrubs. This is best done in winter. Not only will this produce a bare twig as a perch, but it will likely stimulate new growth to improve shelter for possible nest sites below.

Springtime Plantings for Summer, Fall and Winter

Suggested plantings of flower- and seed-producing plants that have value to wildlife appear throughout this book. The wildlife gardener must be selective and, in consultation with local experts in the nursery trade, choose those plants that best suit local environmental conditions. The following chart lists a few weeds and flowers that are attractive to birds.

Transplanting perennials and some biennials, as well as the seeding of annuals, can often be done in either spring or autumn. Your local nursery is the best source of appropriate information. Collecting the seeds of annuals has to be done at the end of the previous flowering season. Storage in a manner to ensure sprouting is often tricky. Once annuals are established, they should self-seed from one year to the next.

For pool, pond or marsh areas the smartweeds (*Polygonum* species) and the pondweeds (*Potamogeton* species) are good seed producers for aquatic birds.

Some Seed-Producing Plants Attractive to Birds

Native Grasses
Panic grass (*Panicum* species)
Crab grass (*Digitaria* species)
Bristle grass (*Setaria* species)

Flowering Plants
Knotweeds (*Polygonum* species)
Pigweeds (*Amaranthus* species)
Lamb's-quarters and Goosefoot (*Chenopodium* species)
Miner's lettuce (*Montia* species)
Chickweeds (*Cerastium* species)
Ragweeds (*Ambrosia* species)
Dandelions (*Taraxacum* species)
Sunflowers (*Helianthus* annuus) and horticultural/
  agricultural varieties
Thistles (*Cirsium* species)
Cosmos (*Cosmos bipinnatus*) and varieties

CHAPTER 10
Gardening for Summer Birds

As spring warms into summer, the heralding of each new day brings with it a crescendo of bird song—the dawn chorus. Following nest-building and egg-laying, this chorus slowly subsides into the uneasy quiet of late July and August. Then, almost without notice, the first of our summer residents begin to slip quietly southward. Soon, they are only a memory.

The summer solstice marks the end of spring and the beginning of summer. Songbirds time their breeding cycle to coincide with the most favorable weather and abundant food resources—fruits, seeds, berries and insects. However, because summer is the dry season, water soon becomes a limiting factor. The need for water—for both drinking and bathing—can easily be satisfied in our gardens. A nicely planned water source can become a real attraction to summer birds.

A second and somewhat lesser need is a quiet, secluded and protected location where young birds can pass through their adolescence and learn the skills needed for survival.

While summer is noteworthy for its abundance of natural foods, the backyard gardener should be aware of when local berry crops ripen. These are favored by robins and thrushes in particular. In the northwest, the ripening begins with salmonberries in early June. Mountain ash (*Sorbus acuparia*) and hawthorn (*Crataegus* species) ripen in August, and the fruits remain through winter. Fruit-producing species are important food sources for young birds. Tanagers and orioles, for example, become fruit-eating when local fruits are in season. When fruit is not available, these birds are very beneficial in insect control.

Water–The Primary Need of the Summer Season

Next to food, nothing is more attractive to summer birds than a good, safe, shallow source of clean water. While water is essential in every season, birds need water most of all in summer. Most birds drink it, many bathe in it, and a few even dunk their food in it.

Birdbaths

Most of us will have watched a robin taking a bath. The bird shuffles into shallow water and then ruffles its feathers and wings, throwing water in all directions. Hummingbirds and bushtits enjoy flitting through a fine spray. Swallows and flycatchers plop into the surface water in a duck-dive fashion, then rise immediately, often repeating this procedure a number of times. Whatever method birds use, the end result is the same. Like humans, it seems to make them feel clean and good.

A pool/birdbath with dripper—note branches in pool to give small birds protection while drinking.

Birdbaths should be shallow and have gently sloping sides if they are to be used for bathing. A non-skid surface is a second prerequisite. Avoid plastic, metal, fiberglass or other slick surfaces. Slightly roughened concrete is ideal.

Your local garden shop or nursery will have a variety of sizes, shapes and styles of birdbaths. Check them carefully for cracks or flaws. Birdbaths with flat rims and slightly sloping sides that permit a water depth of at least 2 inches (5 cm) are best. Should the bathing area be too deep, you can place a little coarse sand, gravel or a flat rock in the bottom to control the depth.

If you have the time, energy and creative flair, you can easily build an attractive bathing area at a chosen location with a small amount of cement.

As with birdhouses and feeders, the location of a birdbath is very important, especially for smaller birds. Perhaps because bathing is a very active indulgence that is easily noticed, placing a birdbath near shrubbery is important. The shrubbery permits an escape route should a predator suddenly appear. Around one of my garden pools, a shallow embayment is covered by a loose canopy of branches. Chickadees, siskins and crossbills now bathe here regularly. Before the canopy was created, this area was used infrequently.

Another way to improve the use of a birdbath is to elevate it into the branches of a large tree. This will keep it away from predators such as cats. This can be accomplished by placing the bath in a sling and using a pulley to elevate it to the desired height. If a dripping hose can be located above the bath, use should improve considerably.

Clean, clear water can quickly become dirty and contaminated when subject to heavy use. Unmanaged birdbaths will become smelly and/or can harbor transmittable diseases. During periods of hot weather and heavy use, a regular hosing and occasional scrubbing are important. A water source that drips or allows a small volume of fresh water to enter the bath will often be enough to keep the water clean and attractive.

Adding Noise

If water is an attraction, the sound of dripping water can be a magnet, especially to small birds on hot days. Drippers, as these noisemakers are often called, may be created in a number of ways. A slightly loosened faucet (with or without an attached hose) located above the shallow portion of the bath can produce enough noise to attract birds from a considerable distance. A bucket with a small pinhole in the bottom placed above the pool can produce a similar result.

Pigeon Dandruff

If native pigeons use your pool, do not be alarmed if you find a white powder floating on the water surface after a bathing session. This dandruff-like substance is part of the pigeon feather maintenance system. Should a pigeon strike a window with force, a body and wing imprint from this powder will often remain.

Water From an Air Conditioner

The byproduct of air conditioning is water distilled from the air being passed through the air conditioning unit. A few years ago a local tourist information booth had an air conditioner in service, and the water distilled from it was allowed to drip onto a small garden below. The puddle became a mecca for a number of sparrows and warblers.

Why waste this precious commodity? Trap it if you can, and by means of a hose or tube, direct it to a location where it can provide relief for birds, insects and other animals that frequent your yard.

Lawn Sprinklers

Watering lawns to keep them green and soft is an important means of attracting robins, chipping sparrows and other birds to your yard. These watered places become important feeding areas when nearby areas become hard and dry.

Depending on the type of sprinkler, in particular how fine a spray it produces, some birds will actually bathe by flitting through the mist and bumping into the saturated foliage, soaking their plumage in the process. In some instances, bushtits have been observed to become so wet they cannot fly until their feathers dry out.

Dust Baths

Believe it or not—one of our best entertainments at Disneyland in California was watching a small flock of house sparrows that took a dust bath in a small garden right alongside one of the large rides. Unperturbed by people or machinery, the sparrows were having a marvelous time.

Water is not the only substance used by birds for bathing. Grouse, quail and house sparrows are very partial to dust baths. In dry, sheltered locations with loose, fine soils, a scrape will be created in which the birds flop and flutter, allowing the fine particles to sift through their feathers. Just like water, the dust acts as a cleansing agent and discourages external parasites such as lice and mites.

The sheltered sunny side of a building or boulder, a protected bank or the base of a tree are all ideal dusting sites. Once established, dust baths will be used from season to season and from year to year. If you wish to ensure their continued use, top them up with a shovel full of fine dry soil.

Crows—the Food Dunkers

In addition to bathing, crows like to dunk their food in water before eating it. A water source for this purpose should be somewhat deeper than a birdbath, though birdbaths are often used. Smaller birds are wary of crows, so it is desirable to locate the crow's water source away from areas frequented by smaller species.

Feeding Summer Birds

To feed or not to feed birds during the summer months is an interesting question. At this time natural foods are in abundance and research tells us that even during the harshest time of the year, when foods are least plentiful, wild birds prefer to forage for natural foods despite the presence of well-stocked feeders. They may rely on, even depend on artificial food supplies to sustain them, but few utilize these sources exclusively.

Through the summer months, a feeder will always have a few birds in attendance. Perhaps, like children, they wish a quick easy snack! My own experience seems to indicate that with a summer feeder in place, sedentary birds perhaps remain in larger numbers during the following autumn and winter. Summer feeding also attracts a few more birds than might be normal during the summer season.

Anting

Anting is another type of feather maintenance activity used by some songbirds. Anting is not a common activity, but certain birds have selected ant nests where they engage in this activity on a reasonably regular basis. Should you come across a bird anting you may be perplexed—you may even be fooled into thinking it is sick or injured. Crows and jays, in particular, will land on a large ant nest, flatten themselves against the surface and allow the ants to climb all over them. The ants, as a protective measure to ward off the bird, eject a formic acid solution, which has a strong vinegar smell, and this becomes distributed through the bird's feathers. Formic acid and other ant secretions are known to be insecticidal, and it is believed one of the prime purposes of this activity is to rid the bird of ecto parasites.

Oranges for Orioles

The northern oriole is not found in all regions, but where it occurs its vivid orange, black and white plumage makes it unmistakable. For its color alone it is a welcome, if not highly prized, visitor to any garden. Orioles are largely frugivorous, which means fruit-eating. Attract them into your garden by placing sectioned oranges into the forks of branches as high up as you can conveniently place them.

Goldfish for Kingfishers and Herons

While it might seem inhumane, you can attract piscivorous (fish-eating) predators to your garden by supplying them with their appropriate foods. In fact, almost every garden pool with fish will become a target for herons and kingfishers. Herons are silent and sneaky; kingfishers are bold, announcing their presence through loud rattling calls.

Having a well-stocked pool is not a lot different from having a well-provisioned bird feeder. The activity around a feeder often becomes a magnet to Cooper's and sharp-shinned hawks and occasionally small owls. A pool becomes the destination for another group of predators.

Many people who have garden pools grimace, with good reason, at the mention of great blue herons or belted kingfishers. These birds steal their prized goldfish! In the aquarium trade most pet stores sell feeder fish in bulk, goldfish that are fed to carnivorous, larger aquarium fish. For a few dollars, a bulk purchase will stock your pool for a season. Some may even survive for a number of years. Such a purchase could be considered a modest investment towards the stately presence of a heron or the rattle of a kingfisher some quiet morning. One thing I can tell you from personal experience is that the white goldfish often disappear first, the orange next and the black ones last—an interesting lesson in natural selection on the basis of color.

Preening

The maintenance of a bird's feathers is an important element in survival. The large body feathers give the bird an aerodynamic shape, underlying feathers provide insulation and the large wing feathers permit flight. Keeping these in fine working order requires regular care and maintenance.

Just above the base of most birds' tails is a large oil-secreting gland known as the preen gland. Birds regularly rub their bills through this patch of feathers to pick up oil that is then transferred to other feathers. The oil waterproofs the feathers and keeps them pliable and strong. This activity, known as preening, is often observed while birds are perching.

CHAPTER 11
Gardening for Autumn Birds

The days shorten and the nights grow cooler, and excitement grips the air as our native birds bunch up in preparation for their southern migration. Restlessness and a degree of nervousness pervade the mixed flocks that gather around abundant food sources. Following the breeding season their quest becomes one of survival—surviving until the next breeding season.

Some time ago the bickering of a multitude of birds in some nearby yew trees sparked a curiosity that led to one of those memorable, serendipitous outdoor experiences. In the trees overhead, nearly a dozen different kinds of birds were feasting, gorging themselves on the red ripe berries of the female yew trees (see photo, next page). Patience and careful observation revealed a much more fascinating story. Yes, it was a banquet of sorts, and yes, many of the birds were feeding, but each type of bird was feeding in quite a different manner.

The robins and thrushes simply plucked and ate the pulp and seed together. Western tanagers ate only the fruit pulp, carefully leaving the skin and seed to drop to the forest floor. Chickadees plucked the seed capsule from within the fleshy arils and promptly spit out the seed. Evening grosbeaks also ate only the seeds after shearing away the flesh and cracking the kernel in their massive bills. The remaining birds—sapsuckers, juncos, siskins and nuthatches—may have been attracted by the noise and commotion. I never observed them to feed on the fruits.

Piecing together this puzzle provided an inner satisfaction and the strong indication that each type of bird's feeding methods were quite different.

Not every garden will have a female yew tree loaded with fruit, but careful observation can provide some fascinating insights into the behavior and "personalities" that separate one kind of backyard bird from another.

With the appearance of small flocks of juncos and other northern migrants, we know summer has truly faded into autumn. As the season further chills to winter, supplemental food sources assume greater importance to those individuals that will remain. Autumn is

Only the female yew tree produces berries—a good wildlife food supply.

the season to winterize your garden and prepare for winter needs.

From a songbird's perspective, autumn is *not* the time to clean up your garden! Old flower stems and weed stalks take on a new purpose by providing cover where birds can seek shelter or forage for food. Seed heads that protrude above the blanket of snow are sought-after food sources. A good fall garden clean-up is not beneficial to wildlife, so leave this work until spring!

Some Autumn Chores

1. Ready or build your winter bird feeders.
2. Add additional cover to brush piles and for protection around feeders.
3. Gather preferred natural foods, such as hawthorn, apple or mountain ash, and store them for midwinter use. Freezing them is best.
4. Improve shelter and windbreaks such as hedges and shelter belts.
5. Predator-proof feeding areas by blocking access routes with large mesh screen.
6. Think ahead to spring and summer. Next season's annuals and biennials sprout in autumn. Identifying and saving them will give them a head start in spring.

"Cover"

In a wildlife management sense "cover" generally means the amount of vegetation in a given area. However, biologists have further defined this to include vegetation that affords a place to hide, protection from climatic extremes, and a place for nesting and roosting. Volumes might be written about cover, because the requirements of different species are so variable. In this book, it generally means a place to seek refuge.

Expecting the Unexpected

Migration is a remarkable phenomenon. Advancements in radar technology now allow us to follow small birds over considerable distances. What biologists are learning is inspirational.

Our small birds usually migrate southward at night when sky and weather conditions are favorable. Should unusual weather conditions such as winds, cloud or fog develop, flights are terminated and the would-be migrants drop back to earth, sometimes well off course. During these freak times, many unusual birds can suddenly appear in unexpected locations, much to the delight of bird watchers. However, there is a catch—the bright crisp plumage of spring has now changed dramatically. Autumn might be called the season of small, dull, brown birds that seem impossible to identify. Have patience, practice and persevere! Do not despair—even the experts readily acknowledge this challenge. Nonetheless, keep a sharp eye out. Some very unusual birds turn up in most areas each year.

Spring and fall are the two seasons to expect the unexpected. Should you locate a *very* unusual species and this is confirmed, every birding hot line in the country will soon know about your find. In some instances hundreds (very rarely thousands) of birding "listers" or "twitchers" will descend on the location where a rarity has been spotted, giving little peace to the immediate neighborhood!

Lathing Screen

Also known as stucco wire, this versatile 2 x 2-inch (5 x 5-cm) heavy gauge wire mesh has many uses in a wildlife garden. It can be a protective shield for plants likely to be eaten by deer or rabbits, keep cats and other predators from feeders and screen out larger birds that would monopolize feeding platforms. Building supply outlets sell it in 4-foot-wide (120-cm) rolls (most economical) or sometimes by the lineal measure.

Hopper Feeder

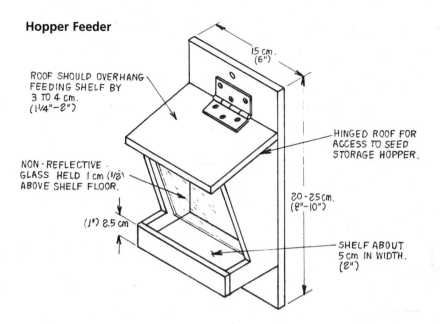

ROOF SHOULD OVERHANG
FEEDING SHELF BY
3 TO 4 cm.
(1¼"–2")

15 cm.
(6")

HINGED ROOF FOR
ACCESS TO SEED
STORAGE HOPPER.

NON-REFLECTIVE
GLASS HELD 1 cm (½")
ABOVE SHELF FLOOR.

(1") 2.5 cm

20-25 cm.
(8"–10")

SHELF ABOUT
5 cm IN WIDTH.
(2")

Bird Feeders

Bird feeders, like birdhouses, can be built in all manner of shapes and sizes. The one overriding consideration for all feeders is to keep the seed as dry as possible. Wet seed will often mildew and spoil. In recent years a number of commercial outlets have begun to specialize in wild bird paraphernalia. Their staff have a great deal of expertise on the subject of bird feeding. A chat with them could be very rewarding and is highly recommended.

In addition to seed dispensers, suet feeders have come into more widespread use in recent years. Prepackaged suet mixtures with hardware holders have somewhat replaced the wire basket or onion bag of old. If you do provide suet, be aware that during spells of mild weather suet can quickly spoil and become rancid.

Woodpeckers use their tails as a prop and need specially constructed feeders they can easily approach. The old standby, a piece of small log with a few large holes drilled into it to hold the suet, is still one of the best and simplest to make.

Seed- and Fruit-Producing Trees and Shrubs Attractive to Birds in Autumn and Winter

Local experts will be able to add a great many more species to this list. On a recent trip to southern Florida, I was impressed by feeding activity at a local shrub, the Brazilian coffee berry. Park managers wanted to see this exotic shrub eliminated, but the catbirds just loved the small red berries.

Native Plants	Introduced Plants
Hawthorns (*Crataegus* species)	English hawthorn (*Crataegus laevigata*)
Crabapple (*Pyrus* species)	Mountain ash (*Sorbus aucuparia*)
Arbutus (*Arbutus menziesii*)	Crabapple (*Malus*, many varieties)
Chokecherry (*Prunus virginiana* and other *Prunus* species)	Holly (female) (*Ilex aquifolium*)
Oaks (*Quercus* species)	Firethorn (*Pyracantha coccinea*, many varieties)
Maples (*Acer* species)	Cotoneaster (*Cotoneaster*, many varieties)
Birches (*Betula* species)	Honeysuckle (*Lonicera* species)
Dogwood (*Cornus* species)	

Building a Good Brush Pile

A brush pile is simply a pile of branches and other natural woody materials, but some care must be taken when constructing it. The purpose is to create some internal space with perches that are a reasonable distance above the ground. A height of 6½ feet (2 m) is ideal.

Begin by selecting six to eight sturdy, reasonably straight, untrimmed branches and arrange them teepee fashion with their butt ends planted firmly into the ground. The branch tips should then mesh, or be woven together. A stout cord may be helpful to hold them together near the top.

On top of this teepee, pile a few evergreen branches, placed with the butts up and the needles pointing downward. This outer shell will break the wind while shedding rain to the outside. Each year add a few more evergreen branches to keep it operational. If the brush pile is started in the spring, climbing plants, such as scarlet runner beans, honeysuckle, clematis, morning glory, or even squash, pumpkin or gourds, can be planted to grow over the pile, for an attractive and practical decoration. In the fall, cornstalks make a good addition to the outside of the pile.

If left open on one side (away from the direction of prevailing winds), brush piles are good feeding areas for small, ground-frequenting birds. A circle of lathing screen will keep cats and other ground predators at bay.

The Bramble Patch

The stoutly armed Himalayan and evergreen blackberries (*Rubus procerus* and *R. laciniatus*) provide nearly impenetrable tangles of dense vegetation that offer ideal cover for songbirds and other wildlife. In addition to good safe cover, the ripe fruit is actively sought by a number of birds and small mammals.

Despite these considerable benefits, the disadvantage of having a blackberry patch in the average garden lies in keeping these invasive, fast-growing vines in check. Since new shoots may grow 17 feet (5 m) or more in a season and root systems are difficult to eradicate, few gardeners may wish to live with these robust plants.

Listers and Twitchers

Birdwatchers keep all kinds of lists—day lists, location lists, garden or property lists—from which they get the name "lister." A "twitcher" has been defined as an archetypal birdwatcher. When these individuals see a species they quickly tick (twitch) it off and move on to the next. Whatever the term, recording or listing species you see in your garden is a worthy endeavor.

CHAPTER 12
Gardening for Winter Birds

Few activities bring people more enjoyment than feeding birds during our dull winter months. For many people in northern areas, the first snowfall means putting out a little food for the birds. In areas with little or no snow, feeding birds brings the same enjoyment, but there is a different cast of characters.

Christmas Bird Counts (CBCs), are conducted in virtually every North American community (and many other countries around the world). Started just over 100 years ago, these annual censuses record as many as 160 species in south Texas, 140 species along the west coast, 120 species through the northeast and the northern prairies and just three or four in the high Arctic. Feeder counts have now become an integral part of this activity. Without even having to leave the comfort of home, people can participate.

Winter is the time when only the hardiest bird species remain in the north. Food and shelter—shelter becoming more important further north—are the two primary needs. Providing different foods, often at different locations, will attract a wider range of species and help separate the larger and smaller birds, avoiding unfair competition.

Hardy evergreen trees that develop thick foliage and shed rain and snow away from the trunk are ideal for providing cover from prevailing winds and for overnight roosting. Spruce trees (*Picea* species) and true firs (*Abies* species) which tend to have flattened branches and needles that act as shingles, are good choices. Balsam fir in the east and grand fir in the west are two that come to mind.

Operating a Winter Feeding Station

There is therapeutic value in having an active bird feeder. You can sit and watch it for hours as the parade of individuals and species succeed one another—an avian soap opera, complete with villains and saints. From this perspective, birds around a window feeder, like fish in your dentist's aquarium, offer relaxation—a commodity not to be underestimated.

A feeding station is a supplemental food source at which our winter birds will spend varying amounts of time. Some individuals become addicted and will always be present. Those that are more independent and prefer to forage for naturally occurring foods will only be transients. Whatever the case, once a feeding program is well underway it should continue through the winter months, in particular, until natural foods are again readily accessible. In times of severe weather, a well-stocked and protected feeding station may well be essential to a small bird's survival.

To be effective, a feeding station does not have to cater to every species likely to be found in your area. One feeder supplied with sunflower seeds and a second with a mix of seeds, such as millet or other small grains, should reap the greatest rewards. If, along with these, a piece of suet or a suet pack (now available commercially) is hung out, you will be catering to the majority of the species found around your garden.

When you change or diversify the menu, you change and diversify your clientele! Four or five feeding stations, each with a different offering, will attract a good variety of bird species. The final consideration may be how much time you wish to spend catering to birds and/or how deep your pockets are.

Keeping Food Dry

Keeping bird foods dry, particularly seed grains, is very important. Wet seed quickly develops molds, which increases the risk of diseases. For this reason, do not hesitate to sweep off or clean out your feeder at each replenishing.

Three measures to keep your seed offering as dry as possible are using feeders with a good overhanging roof; placing your feeder in a sheltered location protected from prevailing winds or driving rain; and using a fine screen as the feeding platform. This latter feature, which may require support rods to prevent the screen from sagging, allows seed to dry quickly should it get wet. Drifting powder snow is a common problem.

Just like a baseball umpire dusting off home plate I carry a 2-inch (5-cm) paint brush and a small putty knife or scraper in my hip pocket. Before I replenish my feeders with fresh seed, I dust or scrape away all the old, loose or possibly contaminated seed. This practice not only ensures a clean feeding station but also extends the longevity of wooden feeders.

Salmonella is a bacterial infection that can be lethal to small birds. Pine siskins and the small finches appear to be most prone, sometimes dying in numbers during late winter. Keeping feeders clean and seed dry are most important to prevent infection. Wooden table-type feeders are most prone to *Salmonella*. They can be sterilized by washing them with a solution of one part household bleach to nine parts water.

Winter Bird Food Preferences

Studies conducted across North America reveal that there are striking differences in the attractiveness of the different foods we put out for our wild birds. What is popular in one area is less attractive in another. In the end, it is the birds that make the choice and it is we who must experiment to find out what works best in our gardens. Sunflower and Niger seed are always near the top of the list, and buckwheat, hulled oats and rice are near the bottom. However, when there is little food around, anything is appreciated.

The variety of products available can make selecting the best bird seed difficult, but knowing these preferences can help in selecting a good seed mix. When you watch towhees scratch away unwanted seeds, or siskins selectively pick out every fifth sunflower seed, you will begin to understand. Getting the best value for your bird-feeding dollar is never simple!

During the winters of 1988 to 1992 I expanded my earlier study of bird food preferences in Nanaimo, British Columbia, from five to 14 commercially available bird seeds. In addition I conducted two summer tests. More than

What Is a 'Good' Wild Bird Feeder Mix?

This is a question that could be debated endlessly. A mix that contained 30% black oil and 10% striped sunflower seed, 30% peanut halves and hearts, 20% red and 5% white millet, and 5% milo would be my choice.

13,000 observations were recorded of 28 species. My findings are presented here in simplified form.

Seed type	Dark-eyed Junco N=3667	Rufous-sided Towhee N=862	Chestnut-backed Chickadee N=158	Song Sparrow N=442	House Finch N=1456	Pine Siskin N=227	Red-winged Blackbird N=1161	Starling N=617
Millet	8%	5%		17%	+		47%	3%
Milo	21%	30%		13%	+	1%	4%	3%
Safflower	1%	+		2%	11%		3%	3%
Sunflower Hulled	23%	1%		4%	7%		1%	
Striped	3%	22%	1%	3%	10%	3%	6%	+
Black	11%	19%	11%	20%	58%	15%	13%	2%
Peanut Hearts	16%	5%	2%	8%	+		+	11%
Halves	5%	8%	86%	2%	+		5%	46%
Hemp	1%	5%		12%	8%		4%	2%
Niger	4%	3%		11%	5%	80%	1%	2%
Chick Scratch	7%	1%		8%	+		17%	28%

N = Number of observations made. + = Less than .5%.

Some Common Commercially Available Bird Foods

Chick Scratch

This commonly available product is a mixture of cracked corn and cracked wheat. The seeds have be fractured to make them smaller and more easily handled by chicks and small birds. Among the sparrows and juncos it is a reasonably popular item, but in the presence of hulled or oil-type sunflower seed, chick scratch is often passed over.

In what would generally be considered poor-quality bird seed mixes, chick scratch and/or finely cracked corn are used as fillers to reduce the price of the mix. Cracked corn is a good food to attract red-winged blackbirds, pheasants and quail.

Millet

These small, round seeds come in a number of varieties. White, red and German millet are among the most common. All are very shiny, smooth-coated seeds that are slippery and flow easily. Milo is a larger, 1/8-inch (2- to 3- mm) seed that is similar, but has a dull coat.

Both millet and milo are commonly added to bird seed mixes as fillers, but both form an important part of the winter diet of sparrows, towhees and juncos that visit bird feeders.

Niger Seed

Niger is expensive when compared to the other seeds, but these small, black seeds are a favorite with goldfinches, siskins and juncos. Dispense them from one of the hanging tube-style feeders.

Sunflower Seeds

Perhaps sunflowers seeds are the best all-round winter bird seed available on the market today. Two general varieties are available, the larger striped and the small all-black oil seeds. For most smaller birds with their somewhat smaller beaks, the oil type is the one preferred hands down. Purple finches and evening grosbeaks prefer the larger striped seeds.

Chickadees and nuthatches like to carry away the smaller seeds either to hide them for future use or to crack and eat them at a location where they won't be intimidated by larger, bullying and more numerous species.

One of the drawbacks to feeding sunflower seeds is the mess. Husks litter the feeder platform and ground after each feeding session. If this is a problem, hulled sunflower seeds and "chips" are available at a somewhat greater cost.

Whole Wheat

Cracked wheat has been discussed previously, but whole wheat is a very reasonably priced bird food that is ideal for some of our larger species. Juncos regularly visit band-tailed pigeon feeders along the west coast to "steal" wheat put out for the pigeons. Ring-necked pheasants and quail also enjoy wheat and/or corn.

Peanuts and Peanut Hearts

Peanuts can be fed to wild birds in a variety of ways—whole, in halves or as peanut hearts. The heart is that little kernel that often breaks away from the halves when they are split. Companies that make peanut butter like to remove the hearts, as it is believed they impart a sour taste to their product. These hearts are then made available to farmers as cattle food or to bird feed suppliers. Peanut hearts have proven to be particularly popular with sparrows. Finches also eat them on a small but regular basis. Peanut halves are selected over hearts by chickadees and nuthatches.

Unshelled peanuts are hoarded by jays who, if allowed, will carry away and stash more peanuts than they will ever eat. For this reason, I recommend a rationing system, where a few peanuts are placed out each or every other day, just enough to keep these colorful, intelligent birds coming back.

Peanut Butter

Peanut butter is an important component of many bird food recipes where its sticky texture is changed by adding ingredients that absorb oil. This sticky consistency, which can be a problem for birds to handle, is further reduced when it's placed outside in a cool environment. Ingredients that can be added to absorb oil include rolled oats, cornmeal and chick scratch. In this harder state, birds are better able to peck off small pieces and swallow them without harm.

Suet

While true suet is the best animal fat to feed wild birds due to its granular nature, it is seldom available from your butcher. In fact, it is usually removed at the packing house. The next best thing is "cod fat." Ask your butcher for this by name, and if there is none available he or she will probably provide you with a suitable substitute, hopefully at no cost. In this day of prepackaging, large modern supermarkets no longer cut their own meat but sell prepackaged suet cubes. For larger pieces you may have to seek out a butcher who sells beef in sides and quarters.

Bread and Kitchen Scraps

Table scraps are often set out for wild birds, though they are not readily accepted by the smaller species. Jays, crows, starlings, house sparrows and gulls certainly enjoy these, and what is left over will be eaten by whatever mammals are in your area. These species may not be the most desirable ones, but they can provide a lot of entertainment.

Feeding birds bread during severe weather is only better than feeding them nothing at all. When compared to the commercially available seed grains, bread has much less food value.

Pecking Order

Every active feeding station will develop a hierarchy that is quite easy to observe. There are two types of competition: between species and between individuals of the same species. Both determine an order of dominance that is known as a pecking order.

In response to this order, a number of species have developed strategies that allow them to beat the system. These are the ones at or near the bottom. Just watch the nuthatches or chickadees. Their strategy is to sneak in, grab a seed and take off. It is comical to watch.

Here is a west coast feeder pecking order.

• Rufous-sided towhee
• Song sparrow
• Pine siskin
• House finch
• Dark-eyed junco
• Chestnut-backed chickadee
• Red-breasted nuthatch

Types of Bird Feeders

There are probably as many styles of bird feeders as there are people who feed birds. For the seed and suet eaters, there are two main types, tube and suet feeders. Each is selective to those species that are able to access them. Tray and hopper feeders allow all species access.

Garden stores, wild bird specialty shops and a number of catalog sale outlets offer a wide variety of feeders. When selecting a feeder, know the species of bird for which the feeder is intended, their food preferences and where and how they prefer to feed.

Tray and Hopper Feeders

Tray and hopper feeders are the open feeders that provide a flat, table-like surface on which the food is presented. The style can be modified in a number of ways to meet local situations and personal preferences. The addition of a hopper allows a supply of seed to be made available a little at a time, saving both time and the bother of constant replenishing. (See diagram in Chapter 11, page 103.)

These types of feeders can be modified to make them selective by adding a visor of lathing screen (see photo, page 102) to keep out larger birds.

Selective Feeders (Tube and Suet Feeders)

Selective feeders include the popular tube-style feeder that hangs from a branch, pole or eavestrough. It has short perches that make it difficult or impossible for larger birds to gain access. Chickadees, siskins, goldfinches and like-sized birds are particularly adept at using these. A broad protective roof is a good feature for locations with wet or snowy weather. The best seeds for tube feeders are the small black sunflower and Niger seeds. Wild bird mixes tend to clog tube feeders in damp conditions.

Many of the suet feeders designed for woodpeckers have a degree of selectivity. Species that are unable to cling to a vertical surface of the hole-type feeders are excluded, though some of these will certainly try to get at the suet.

Locating Your Feeder

Around a feeding station each species has a preferred route of approach (see illustration, page 114) and a preferred feeding method. For instance, juncos and song sparrows sit and pick, while chickadees grab and run. House finches like to drop in from an overhead perch. Keeping these behaviors in mind, a few other considerations for locating feeders include visibility of the feeders from your home, shelter from prevailing winds and weather, and availability of nearby cover to escape from predators. In choosing an appropriate location, these factors need to be balanced.

Winter Birds Not Attracted to Feeders

While many winter species find feeders hard to resist, there are a few that seldom make an appearance. In my experience these include the golden-crowned kinglets and brown creepers. Both are insect gleaners that, unlike other members of their guild, the chickadees and nuthatches, appear not to have learned to utilize bird feeders even if peanut pieces and sunflower seeds are offered. Surely, among the varieties of food and recipes available, there is one delicacy that might tempt these interesting species?

Placing feeders in the open, where we can see them easily, leaves the users vulnerable. Feeders for small birds should be placed as near cover as possible. Better still, tuck them away slightly within vegetation. A few branches that extend beyond the feeder not only provides convenient perches and foils predators.

A nearby clump of tall shrubs or a small tree with a few bare branches near the top make good lookouts.

Winter Bird Food Recipes

Nearly every person who regularly feeds birds in his or her backyard has favorite recipes for the feathered visitors. Generally speaking, these recipes are a mixture of two ingredients: fat, usually as suet or peanut butter, and seed grains. Fruits, kitchen scraps and bread are a few other ingredients used frequently.

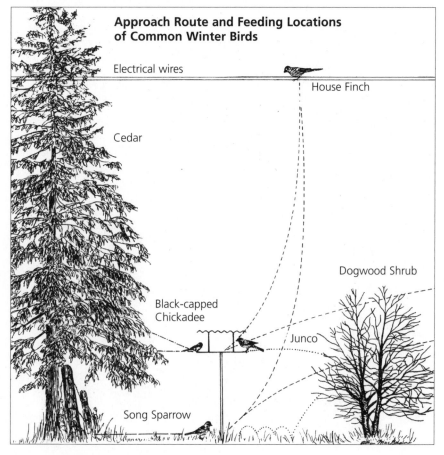

Approach Route and Feeding Locations of Common Winter Birds

Electrical wires

House Finch

Cedar

Dogwood Shrub

Black-capped Chickadee

Junco

Song Sparrow

For exotic seeds, contact a shop that caters to cage bird enthusiasts.

While I was working on this manuscript, a flock of bushtits provided an enjoyable diversion as they buzzed around a mixture of drippings, peanut butter and rolled oats. This stiff paste had been pushed into 2-inch (5-cm) holes in a section of tree trunk. I left side branches to provide perches for the whole flock.

The recipes included here are but three of many that have appeared over the years. Feel free to experiment.

Please remember that fats become rancid in warm weather. Putting these out only during the cooler months may prevent birds from soiling their feathers as they feed. Avoid bacon grease—the salt content is very high.

Nuthatch and Chickadee Balls
Cut up or grind 1 pound (455 g) of suet. Heat slightly until the suet softens and becomes sticky. Stir in about a cup (250 mL) of whole or hulled sunflower seeds (hulled are the best) so the mixture becomes stiff. Roll the mixture into 2-inch (5-cm) balls and cool in a refrigerator or freezer. Hang out in a mesh bag as needed.

Woodpecker Mix
Ingredients:
1 part (by volume) peanut butter
2 parts melted suet
2 parts cornmeal
4 parts finely cracked corn (or chick scratch)

Mix all the ingredients together and push portions of the mixture into a hole feeder, or stuff it into cracks or holes in a log, snag or stump.

The Crawford Bird Food Recipe
Ingredients:
1 cup (250 mL) of sugar
3 cups (750 mL) water
1 pound (455 g) suet
1/2 cup (125 mL) peanut butter
1 cup (250 mL) dry cream of wheat or oatmeal

Combine the water and sugar, bring to a boil and add the suet. Mix in the peanut butter, add the cereal component and allow the mixture to cool. If mixture remains too soft, add more dry cereal until a thick consistency is achieved.

Roll the mixture into balls and place in an onion string bag or wire screen container. You can also force the mixture between the scales of a large pine cone and hang it outside with a piece of wire (squirrels will chew through string). An alternative is to pour the warm soft mixture into a large fruit juice tin and push the cone into this mixture. When it has hardened slightly, pull out the cone.

Providing Water in Winter

Birds appreciate water, even during the coldest periods of the year, for drinking and bathing. In northern areas freezing can be a problem. It takes 80 calories to melt .03 ounce (1 gram) of ice. This is a lot of energy for a small bird, whose sole water source may be snow, to generate. One way to solve this dilemma is to use a small-wattage electric light bulb or a short length of electric heat tape. To keep the heat tape stationary and submerged, wrap it around a short piece of pipe. (See illustration below.) Thermostatically controlled heaters, suitable for use in birdbaths, are now available commercially. These are capable of providing fresh water even during the coldest weather.

Just as it is in summer, replenishing and keeping the water supply clean is an important practice for all artificial water sources.

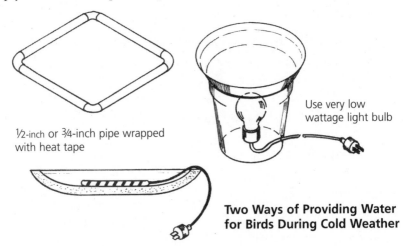

½-inch or ¾-inch pipe wrapped
with heat tape

Use very low
wattage light bulb

**Two Ways of Providing Water
for Birds During Cold Weather**

CHAPTER 13
Wildlife Gardening on Balconies and Patios

Some years ago when visiting Montreal, my accommodations in the heart of the city offered a view of a most impressive neighboring patio garden. Though small and compact, it was a creation of beauty. It was also a poignant reminder that even where concrete and asphalt are the rule, a person with a green thumb and a little creativity can reap the considerable benefits of a small oasis. Just because some people prefer to live in an apartment or a condominium they need not be excluded from enjoying an association with some of the common species of urban wildlife.

Many building owners frown on or even establish rules prohibiting the feeding of birds from windows or balconies. Nonetheless, there are many simple practices that can render these types of residences much less sterile. After all, if a hummingbird finds your fuschia attractive, or a house finch decides to nest in your potted shrub or hanging flower basket, can the occupant be blamed?

Imagine the following situation, which happened locally in a sixth-floor, downtown apartment.

One afternoon in early spring, the occupant arrived home to find that a pair of Canada geese had taken over a planter on his balcony! Amused at first, he watched the pair pull together their nest. Then six eggs appeared, and by this time he no longer had the heart to evict his new tenants. After all, a Canada goose gander is not a bird many people would wish to confront, let alone try to evict from an established nest site.

An impasse arrived some weeks later when the eggs hatched. By this time, the balcony-nesting geese had become a hot news item for the local press, television and radio media. With backup from media personnel, and with the gander temporarily absent, a quick raid netted the female goose and her six goslings. Via the elevator, they were removed and relocated to a nearby park with a small pond. All that remained was the balcony clean-up and planter restoration!

Amid the concrete and glass skyscrapers and the asphalt and concrete roadways of many of our large cities, the cheerful call of the house finch can now be heard on quiet spring mornings. Its presence is a reflection of city programs to "green up" the downtown core. Nesting and roosting sites are found among the clinging vines and cascades of hanging shrubs that dress up these public areas. As this greening continues, who knows what other songbirds might appear?

Due to their mobility, birds are the wildlife group most easily appreciated by apartment dwellers, but the variety of species likely to be observed from windows and balconies will be quite restricted. Birds most likely to be present include the house sparrow, rock dove, European starling, one or two varieties of gulls and, depending on location, either the common or northwestern crow. To many people these are some of our less desirable species, but regardless of personal bias, they deserve our admiration. Not only do they survive, even thrive, in a difficult environment, they also endure considerable hostile public opinion. And when their interesting qualities are appreciated, they can bring the watcher many hundreds of hours of enjoyment in situations where few other wildlife distractions may be present.

Although the species listed above are the most commonly seen birds in cities, there are others. Chimney swifts (in eastern regions), the common nighthawk, the occasional swallow and peregrine falcons have all taken to city environments. Further, during migration periods in early spring and autumn, any number of

Some Plants for Balconies and Window Gardens

- Window and railing boxes, hanging baskets
  - Fuchsias
  - Alyssums
  - Chrysanthemums and daisies
  - Columbines
  - Nasturtiums
- Pots and tubs
  - **Shrubs**
    - Columnar cedar
    - Mugho pine
  - **Vines**
    - Clematis
    - Scarlet runner beans

songbird species may come back to earth in unexpected places. Nicely planted balconies, rooftop gardens or other patches of vegetation may become short-term resting places until the next leg of the migration begins. Remember too, a number of colorful butterflies also migrate, and an incredible diversity of insect species—as well as gray squirrels—seem to get just about everywhere.

Many of the ideas presented in the previous chapters can be adapted or tailored for use near windows or on balcony and rooftop gardens.

Shelter

Of the three needs—shelter, water and food—on which all species depend, shelter is the hardest for the apartment dweller to provide. This will depend to a degree on how far above the ground your balcony or window is. A few nearby trees are helpful in providing a jumping-off point for many of the smaller birds that might visit balconies for a feed or drink.

Tapestry walls—vertical gardens built against a sturdy wall—may afford a temporary green haven for small species. Behind a lining are pockets of soil (See illustration below) in which the plants are rooted. By carefully selecting plants for their color, foliage and texture you can produce a very attractive wall—to humans as well as birds, butterflies and insects. (See the plant list in the chapters

Construction Details for a Tapestry Wall

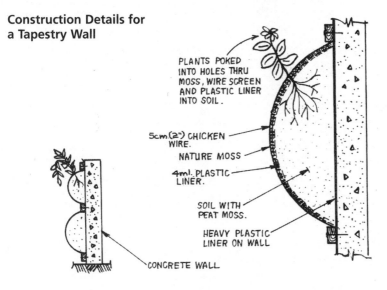

PLANTS POKED INTO HOLES THRU MOSS, WIRE SCREEN AND PLASTIC LINER INTO SOIL.

5cm.(2") CHICKEN WIRE.

NATURE MOSS

4ml. PLASTIC LINER.

SOIL WITH PEAT MOSS.

HEAVY PLASTIC LINER ON WALL

CONCRETE WALL

that deal with these species.) Like all potted plants, tapestry walls require regular watering and attention.

A tapestry wall may also be an appropriate addition to walkways, patios, building walls or similar bare vertical surfaces.

A Nest Box for Swallows or House Sparrows

Violet-green or, occasionally, tree swallows sometimes frequent built-up areas of cities. These species, which seldom settle on the ground, do quite well in downtown environments. If they can find a small opening or crack in a building's facade that opens into a cavity large enough for nesting, they likely will stick around through spring and summer. Updrafts carry the small flying insects on which these species feed. Even higher overhead are the chimney swifts (central plains and eastward), which, true to their name, often glue their nest to the inside flue of a chimney.

If you are lucky enough to have swallows around your apartment, you may be able to encourage their nesting with a suitable nest box (see Chapter 9). If house sparrows are in your vicinity, a bluebird-sized nest box will cater to this species.

Water

Water can be provided manually or be a byproduct of your air conditioner during the hot summer months. While a full-sized birdbath may be too large, a small, attractive water source for sipping or food dunking, in the case of crows, could be considered. If a dripper can be set up, the motion and sound are very attractive to birds.

If you have a larger balcony or a patio, you can successfully grow water lilies and other water plants in a barrel or in a half barrel, if weight is a concern. These types of planters require a good sunny exposure. Once the garden has been planted, goldfish and other pond animals, such as snails, can be added. Where freezing is a possibility the tubs need to be protected or brought indoors.

Food

By necessity, balcony and window feeders will have to be small. In most cases a flat surface is all that is required. Should you wish to feed large and small birds from the same feeder, the upper tray for the large birds can act as the roof of the one for the small birds

Hanging feeders, a clothes-line feeder or a suet bag are simple and easy to maintain.

Discarded sunflower seed shells and spilled seed can be a messy problem around feeding areas. One way to minimize the problem is to put out only sunflower seed chips, thereby eliminating the messy husks.

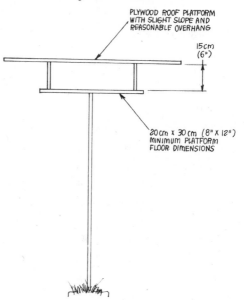

A Two-Storey Bird Feeder

PLYWOOD ROOF PLATFORM WITH SLIGHT SLOPE AND REASONABLE OVERHANG

15cm (6")

20cm x 30cm (8" x 12") MINIMUM PLATFORM FLOOR DIMENSIONS

Food Preferences of Downtown Birds

Bird	Foods
Gulls	Kitchen scraps
Rock doves	Wheat, rice, dried bread
Crows	Kitchen scraps, fruits, whole nuts
European starlings	Suet, food scraps, peanut pieces, fruits
House sparrows	Chick scratch, dried breadcrumbs, small grains
House finches	Sunflower seeds (small black preferred), safflower and small peanut pieces or peanut hearts; also like to drink at hummingbird sugar-water feeders

Sugar Water for House Finches

Hummingbird feeders are often visited by house finches that appear to have a distinct preference for sweetened water. Farm supply stores sell a chick fount. This simple dispenser (a bottle of water turned upside down in a shallow dish might be made to work in the same way) filled with a one to four mixture (by volume) of white granulated sugar to water may entice house finches to become regular visitors. You will need small quantities only—larger amounts will spoil before they're used.

The Feeder Pole

Those who have visited Asian cities may have noted how families in some multistorey buildings hang out their laundry to dry. A long bamboo pole is used to extend the washing out away from their balcony and over the street. With many hundreds of washing poles out at any one time, the sight is quite impressive. Bird feeders can be extended away from the building in the same manner. This may take the feeder closer to nearby trees, for cover, or, by getting the feeder away from a building, greatly reduce the possibility of mess, or discoloration, that their activities could create.

CHAPTER 14

Planning Your Wildlife Garden

Good wildlife gardens don't just happen—they take careful planning, considerable work and much refinement. Planning is the carefully thought-out, orderly provision of shelter, food and water to maximize a garden's attractiveness to urban wildlife. The process can be divided up into a number of functions, including site selection, site analysis, drawing up a rough or conceptual plan, making a final plan and building your garden. Planning concludes when you have created your garden and evaluated the results, but in reality planning never really ends for most people—new ideas continually come to mind and are incorporated into the existing garden scheme.

The first step in the process is site selection. Unless you are purchasing a home or property, this part of the process will be a given. Many of us inherit our gardens from a previous owner, in which case we will be concerned largely with the remaining planning stages. This is where we consider the what, where, why and how.

It is always helpful in the beginning to put ideas down on paper, although few of us really do this. Most of us are content to work from a concept that is simply an image in our heads. However, having gone through this exercise a number of times, I find it to be a helpful practice to have something on paper—even when the final result differs from what was first envisaged.

Site Analysis

This stage involves the inventory and evaluation of the physical features already on site. As you walk around your property, record the location and size of the following.

- Property boundaries and fence lines.
- Footprint of buildings (residence, garage and/or storage sheds); decks, patios, pools, sidewalks and paths.
- Existing trees, shrubs, flower beds and vegetable gardens.
- Stumps, boulders, rock piles, embankments and ditches.
- Natural water courses, water tap locations and downspouts from roofs.
- Avenues with good views from residence windows, to be kept unobstructed, and poor views that require screening.

Mark the following features, which are also important when planning.

- Topography—showing rough elevations of hills and hollows.
- Water and sewer lines, drains and underground tanks.
- Power lines and telephone cables, overhead or underground.
- Prevailing wind direction.
- Direction of exposure to the sun.

A Rough Plan

Once you have a firm idea of your property with all its assets and limitations, it is time to draw up the rough plan. Here are some concepts to keep in mind.

Edges

One biological concept that is well documented for its importance to wildlife, particularly birds and mammals, is the value of *edges*. The interface between open space and dense vegetation is the area favored by most wildlife. It is along these transitions that wildlife is most easily observed.

While the average city garden generally will not have enough area to create significant edges, by planting the tallest and densest trees—usually evergreens—around the perimeter and shrubs towards the inside, you can create an interesting edge zone. To develop such an edge from scratch may take many years. In planning and developing, consider diversity in both height and breadth of your plantings, and try to maximize both. As time passes thinning may be in order. If your property abuts a ravine or other natural area, or a public domain, incorporate its natural occurring vegetation into your long-term plan. Also consider neighboring properties. They could be developed some time in the future, and it is never too soon to establish hedges and screens for personal privacy or improved wildlife values.

Wildlife Corridors

Wildlife, particularly medium-sized mammals such as raccoons, skunks, coyotes and foxes, have fairly large territories within which they live and travel. While on their rounds they follow somewhat regular routes or pathways, and tracts of vegetation that follow streams, ravines and breaks in the landscape serve as wildlife corridors. Parklands, green belts, railway lines, highway corridors—even culverts—are access routes by which animals travel safely from one part of their territory to another. If your property abuts a wildlife corridor it is an advantage when planning a wildlife garden.

Zoning

Because all species of wildlife are not always compatible, you may wish to consider zoning your garden to cater to different species at separate locations. There are many ways this might be accomplished. The following are some examples.

- **Using Behaviour.** At feeding stations, juncos and song sparrows generally prefer to feed on the ground. House

An Axiom Worth Remembering

It takes diversity to reap variety. In other words, the greater and more varied the features you can incorporate into your garden, and the greater the variety of plant species present, the greater should be the variety of wildlife species you can expect to attract.

finches, which enjoy some of the same foods, prefer an elevated feeder.

- **Using Abilities.** Squirrels cannot generally climb metal pipe posts to feeders intended for small birds. Starlings cannot enter birdhouses with holes less than 1½ inches (4 cm) in diameter, whereas swallows can. Peanut chunk feeders, screened with lathing screen, are not accessible to pigeons, jays and many of the medium-sized birds, but are open to nuthatches and chickadees.

- **Using Food Preferences.** Starlings do not show much interest in bird feeders that offer the small seeds or sunflower seed preferred by most of the smaller birds.

- **Using Time.** Food put out at dusk will be available to flying squirrels and raccoons while daytime feeders, such as grosbeaks and crows, are roosting.

These are just a few of many ways that a wildlife gardener can add a degree of control to the activities in the garden. This list is not exhaustive; careful observation will reveal more ways in which zoning might be helpful.

Avenues of View

One of the major considerations of the wildlife garden is to be able to see the birds and other creatures from your windows. Therefore, in the conceptual planning stage, make sure that you provide and maintain good sight lines into the corners of your garden.

Consider whether the plan or layout of your house, even your activity patterns, can focus on the concept of viewing avenues. Second-story windows are particularly good vantage points. A work space, such as a sewing table, writing desk or computer station, positioned with a view may allow two interests to coincide.

Water Sources and Garden Lighting

The provision of water sources, such as drippers for birdbaths, pools or sprinkling systems, should be thought out early in the process, as should lighting and underground wiring.

Drawing Up the Rough Plan

Now that you have analyzed your property and your ideas are clear, it is time to formulate a rough plan. You can sketch it onto paper or a chalkboard. Some people use cut-outs of the features and plantings, which they shuffle around the space available. This allows you to try out different configurations. If each object is to scale, it is a great help when drawing up the final plan.

The Final Plan

When you have all your ideas sorted out, draw up your final plan on a sheet of graph paper. Keeping features to scale will give you a much better perspective of how your ideas fit in relation to one another. The illustration, below, is a stylized plan indicating the general arrangement for a typical backyard wildlife garden.

If you can, include contour or elevation lines. Even in a rough form they will be helpful, particularly if someone else will be doing the initial landscaping.

To complete this plan, all that remains is to include the names of the trees, shrubs and flowers you wish to plant. Some of these may come from the lists in this book, and garden centers will be able to help with others known to do well in your area.

Armed with the detailed plan, it will be much easier to explain your wishes to others, not to mention saving time during actual construction.

Once the contouring, construction of special features and planting are complete, you will have your baseline garden. You may wish to enhance it by providing artificial sources of food, water and shelter.

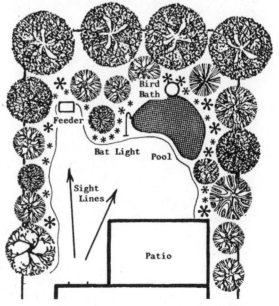

A stylized plan for an average backyard. Tall trees to the outside, shrubs to the inside.

These include feeding stations, nesting or hibernation boxes, pools and lighting.

Evaluation

Just because your garden is constructed does not mean it is finished. Perhaps a wildlife garden is never finished. At this point you cannot sit back and rest on your laurels. Now is the time for constructive criticism and formal evaluation of your masterpiece. From your own observations you may wish to modify your creation, to fine-tune it in order to make it even better. This is a challenge to last a lifetime! See Observing and Keeping Records in Chapter 15 for some helpful information on this aspect of the evaluation process.

A garden with a good "avenue of view."

The old cliché that Rome was not built in a day applies equally to your wildlife garden. But by putting time on your side and exercising patience, time can work for you. In my formative years my father would tell me "little and often." Now, through hindsight, the wisdom of his words rings true.

For heavier tasks, bite off manageable units of work, one at a time. When constructing my "great wall," I tried to put at least 10 large rocks in place each weekend. In half a year, this project was virtually complete. At one unit a day, 365 units can be completed in a year—and we all know how fast a year goes! Persistence and patience will eventually reduce the greatest tasks. If you need a little variety, work on two or three jobs concurrently!

CHAPTER 15

Good Wildlife Gardening Practices

Gardening practices to improve gardens for wildlife are many and varied. Basically they relate to improving the habitat's ability to provide food, shelter and water. Good wildlife gardens need not be, and are best not, precisely laid out, neatly manicured areas. Of course, some order and planning is desirable, as outlined in the previous chapter. Perhaps an appropriate description of a good wildlife garden is one with an untidy order, verging on planned chaos!

Often we overlook or demean some of the most beneficial aspects of gardens. Some years ago, naturalist R. Yorke Edwards of Victoria, B.C., wrote a delightful piece about an old apple tree in his garden. In edited form it is presented here because it provides an uncommon appreciation of backyard gardening.

The oldest, ugliest tree in my garden is the best in my opinion, for it is an apple that every year produces the miracle that someone has named Gravenstein apples.

Give me a Gravenstein, picked warm and perfumed in the autumn sun, and you can have all the leathery skinned Mackintoshes [sic] and every tasteless Delicious apple in the world.

My Gravenstein also gives me an endless crop of pleasure because it is no sterile apple factory. It is a community teeming with life. To me such a variety of life is a more precious and valuable thing than apples, even Gravenstein apples.

When parts of the tree die, the bark loosens and, especially in damp warm weather, the wood lice hide here from the sun. An apple man once told me to get rid of all the loose bark because he said "bugs" hide under it. I didn't tell him that I leave it there for the same reason.

When I pruned off the dead limbs, I left some stubs, hoping for downy woodpeckers. And downys came, made a nursery there, and raised a family. Then for six years running, that apple tree yielded a crop of chestnut-backed chickadees. In the process it also yielded six years of pleasure from my watching.

In summer, the violet-green swallows swoop low over my tree; in the autumn it is the hunting ground for swarms of common bushtits; in winter the house finches sun themselves there on warm days and in February a Bewick's wren begins to proclaim the arrival of spring from a high perch.

On top of this, my Gravenstein gives me blossoms, and shade, and apples.

To recognize that a thing can be good—and worth saving—simply because it is good to look upon, or to listen to, or to smell, or to touch or to think about goes far beyond gains in dollars and cents, amounts of wood or pounds of apples.

Some features, such as sidewalks, fences, patios, pools and hedges, can be precise to the point of being geometric, but many other features, such as composts, brush piles, weed patches, snags and plants with interesting foliage, can counterbalance this regimentation. The result may appear somewhat untidy, but this does not mean that the garden is unmanaged or neglected. After all, weeds and natural litter are favored haunts of many fascinating creatures.

To virtually sterilize a garden through overzealous garden practices, often including liberal applications of herbicides, insecticides and fungicides, eliminates an incredibly diversified cast of characters. *Silent Spring*, Rachel Carson's award-winning treatise, became a wake-up call alerting gardeners to the dangers of these outdated and unnecessary practices.

Common sense, along with an understanding of the basic needs of garden wildlife, should be the guiding principles for gardeners when providing for these animals. The task need not be elaborate, onerous or overly time-consuming. Keeping things simple is an important landmark for success.

Weeds

While gardening enthusiasts often dislike weeds with a vengeance, it should be remembered that a weed is just a "flowering plant growing in the wrong location." Though most weeds do not have the color or foliage of their cultivated counterparts, their value to wildlife should not be underestimated. In a wildlife garden, having a really good weed patch is an asset and not a liability. Selectively encouraging good weeds with wildlife values in a corner of the garden will provide both food and cover. Some good wildlife weeds are listed in the following chart.

Plant	Life Cycle	Comments
Thistles (*Cirsium* species) (*Carduus* species)	Biennial (some perennial)	Favored by butterflies, bumblebees and goldfinches.
Milkweeds (*Asclepias* species)	Perennial	A favorite of butterflies, particularly monarchs.
Lamb's-quarters (*Chenopodium* species)	Annual	Seeds favored by songbirds such as house finches.
Knotweeds and Smartweeds (*Polygonum* species)	Annual	Seeds favored by songbirds and upland game birds.
Chickweeds (*Stellaria* species) (*Cerastium* species)	Annual	Seeds favored by songbirds.
Mullein (*Verbascum* thapsus)	Biennial	Tall flower stalks hold seeds and shelter small insects above snow.
Dandelion (*Taraxacum* species)	Perennial	Seed heads favored by goldfinches and pine siskins.

Developing a Weed Patch

Despite notions to the contrary, weeds do not grow just anywhere. Good wildlife weeds require an open, sunny location, with moist, not soggy, soils of average texture. Once these requirements have been met at a desired location, there are two methods, other than by pure chance, by which the appropriate weeds can become established. You can collect the seed from plants nearby and scatter or shallowly bury it in the fall, or you can transplant seedlings (if you can identify them) to your chosen location in the spring.

For biennial species, like thistles and mullein, that take two years before they flower and set seed, a degree of patience is required. For these, you will need odd- and even-year generations if you desire their presence on a year-to-year basis. Note that creeping Canada thistle (*Cirsium arvense*) and some other weeds with underground runners can become serious nuisances, difficult to eradicate. If you want to have these on your property, planting them in a large container will confine their roaming.

Fruits and Vegetables Attractive to Wildlife

Real conflicts develop over who gets the fruits from a backyard garden. Do they belong to the person who planted and cultivated them or to the animal who gets there first? The outcome is usually a split decision, though the gardener often seems to come out second-best. While all cultivated fruits and vegetables are not equally attractive to wildlife, there are a few that stand out.

When it comes to fruit trees and other vegetables, a healthy bee population will ensure good pollination and improve production. See Chapter 3 for information about mason bees, which are very effective pollinators.

Fruits and Vegetables With Wildlife Values

Type	Comments
Apple (including crabapple)	Fruits left on the tree over winter provide winter food for robins, waxwings and starlings. These trees offer some of the best nesting locations for robins, house finches and chipping sparrows.
Cherry	Produces summer fruit for robins, tanagers, house finches and starlings.
Corn	Summer and autumn food for raccoons, game birds. Stalks stacked teepee-style provide shelter.
Sunflower	Autumn and winter foods for chickadees, grosbeaks and many other birds and small mammals.
Grape	When trained to grow over a trellis, against a wall or over a tall stump, these vines provide good nesting cover for a number of bird species. Note: Riverbank grape (*Vitis riparia*), an escape from cultivation, is known for its vigorous growth.

Quick Solutions for Barren Areas

Waiting for attractive or beneficial trees and shrubs to grow to an appropriate size and form may take a lifetime. Quick solutions are available to fill in gaps or spaces. While these may not be ideal, they buy time while more desirable species are growing. When the preferred species reach sufficient size, the stand-ins can be pruned back, relocated or eliminated. Some fast-growing species for barren areas are listed.

Annual vines such as beans or squash can be allowed to grow over brush piles and stumps. At season's end, leave them to provide additional cover during winter. Replant the following spring if desired.

Mullein Stalks

This robust biennial develops a tall, stiff, often branched flower stalk. In winter the erect dried stalks become foraging areas for chickadees and small woodpeckers. They search for insects that either hide among the seed pods or remain as larvae, pupae or adults feeding on the seeds. One of the common seed nibblers is a small weevil. Growing mullein or bringing a few dead stalks into the garden will often attract insect-searching birds.

Perennial vines, such as clematis, honeysuckle, morning glory and hops, can be trained along fences, trellises and walls. Species that have the ability to cling to structures, such as ivy and Virginia creeper, will not require support.

Quick screens can also be developed by burying the butts of 7- to 10-foot-long (2 to 3 m) branches in the ground to form a hedge and then training vines to grow up and between the supports. Some species of willow, cottonwood and poplar will readily root from a branch stuck in the ground. Caution is advised with these fast-growing species, as the root systems are invasive. Drains or tile fields can be damaged.

Plants for Quick Cover

Trees
Willows (*Salix* species)
Suckers and shoots often root when pushed into soft moist soil. Willows, though messy, are excellent for many forms of wildlife.

Poplar (*Populus* species)
As above. Roots are invasive to water drainage systems. Note: Lombardy poplar (*Populus nigra italica*) is a popular imported tree noted for its columnar growth.

Shrubs
Butterfly bush (*Buddleia davidii*)
Often grows like a weed. Many varieties and flower colors available. Easy to start from cuttings. Pruning improves form and lengthens blooming period.

Weigela (*Weigela* species)
Grows quickly; becomes ragged if not pruned. Many color varieties available.

Fast-Growing Perennial Vines
Clematis (*Clematis* species)
Colorful flowering vines for fences and trellises. Provides cover but wildlife food values minimal.

Virginia creeper (*Parthenocissus quinquefolia*)
Deciduous leaves turn bright red in fall. Fruit attractive to some birds.

Boston ivy (*Parthenocissus tricuspidata*)
A fast-growing evergreen vine that attaches to tree bark and walls. Makes dense cover.

Honeysuckle (*Lonicera* species)
Has double wildlife value—blossoms for hummingbirds in spring and colorful fruits for robins and thrushes in winter.

Hops (*Humulus lupulus*)
Grows quickly but needs rich soil and lots of water. Attracts insects which become bird food.

English ivy (*Hedera helix*)
Evergreen woody vine. Large dense tangles used by raccoons as daytime retreats.

Morning glory (*Ipomoea* species and *Convolvulus arevense*)
Provide shallow tangles of vines with large colorful flowers.

Fast-Growing Annual Vines
Sweet pea (*Lathyrus odoratus*)
Sweet-scented flowers in many colors. Good for screens.

Broad-leaved peavine (*Lathyrus latifolius*)
A perennial pea of roadsides with spikes of colorful white to magenta flowers.

Edible pea (many varieties)
Seeds favored by towhees and game birds. Tall varieties best.

Gourds, pumpkins, squash
May be trained to grow as screens over trellises and brush piles. Seeds eaten by some birds and small mammals.

Hardy Trees and Shrubs With Wildlife Values

Northern and interior parts of North America with a cold, rigorous winter climate offer special challenges for the wildlife gardener. Both wildlife and vegetation must be very hardy. Local nurseries are always the best places to start when looking for information on what to plant in any region. Nursery staff may even know which species are most likely to provide some value to wildlife. The following chart lists a few hardy tree species.

Some Trees and Shrubs for Interior and Northern Locations

Green ash (*Fraxinus pennsylvanica*)
Thrives in moist soils, tolerates severe freezing weather, but foliage burns in hot dry weather.

Black cherry (*Prunus serotina*)
Grows in a variety of soils, producing fruit every three to four years.

Nanking cherry (*Prunus tomentosa*)
A tough, hardy shrub that produces small scarlet fruits.

Silver maple (*Acer saccharinum*)
Fast growing but the limbs and trunk break easily. Tolerates a variety of soils.

Box elder (Manitoba maple) (*Acer negundo*)
Grows in a variety of conditions. Seeds and suckers readily.

Amur maple (*Acer ginnala*)
A hardy shrub or small tree with scarlet autumn foliage.

Russian olive (*Eleagnus angustifolia*)
Fruits that ripen in summer and persist through winter, providing food for wildlife.

Autumn olive (*Eleagnus umbellata*)
Similar to the Russian olive but more shrub-like and sprawling in its form.

Tatarian or Siberian dogwood (*Cornus alba*)
Red-branching shrub that produces small white berries.

Hedges and Hedgerows

Those who have traveled down Old Country roads will be familiar with hedgerows. On this side of the Atlantic, hedgerows are not as common and are replaced in urban environments with trimmed hedges. Both are important to wildlife, particularly in more rural areas.

These thorny tangles are greatly improved as wildlife habitat when interspersed with small trees and the occasional evergreen. Some useful additions include the multiflora rose (*Rosa multiflora*) and Russian olive (*Eleagnus angustifolia*). The following chart lists some of the common small trees and shrubs that have high wildlife values.

Common Small Trees and Shrubs of Hedgerows

Hawthorn (*Crataegus* species)
Both native and introduced species often noted for their long, curved and very sharp spines. Their small fruits are excellent winter bird food.

Crabapple (*Malus* species)
Often multi-stemmed or many-branched, small trees that produce copious quantities of small apples.

Rose (*Rosa* species)
Many species noted for their stout prickles, large sweet-scented flowers and red fruits, known as hips. The small-fruited forms are the ones most favored by wildlife.

Snowberry (*Symphoricarpos* species)
Known for their large, white, soft berries which are eaten infrequently by a variety of birds. The small flowers are often frequented by hummingbirds.

Willow (*Salix* species)
There are a tremendous variety of "pussy willows." Virtually all have con-siderable wildlife values.

Himalayan blackberry (*Rubus discolor*)
Blackberry tangles or briar patches offer ideal refuge to many small birds and mammals. The fruits, even when dry (winter), offer good food value.

Elderberry (*Sambucus* species)
An often irregular, gangly shrub with clusters of red, blue or occasionally black berries.

Litter and Composting

Litter, in the form of leaves, bark and small branches, accumulates in any wild area as part of the natural cycle. Decomposition is a very important part of a healthy ecosystem and is especially crit-ical to many types of wildlife, including wolf spiders, earthworms, salamanders and millipedes. Towhees and fox spar-rows find leaf litter an ideal foraging medium. As the litter decomposes to become a homogeneous part of the soil, it

Making Hedgerows and Garden Thickets Cat-Proof

Probably the greatest danger to birds frequenting backyard gardens is the cat population. To minimize access and ambush sites, try weaving lengths of 2- x 2-inch (5- x 5-cm) lath-ing screen between the upright stems, yet snug to the ground. This allows small birds and mammals to pass through it easily.

provides a multitude of environments characterized by being loose, moist and organic, a haven for small animals. For gardeners, the other side of the coin is the messy appearance litter presents.

Depending on the tree species overhead, which supply the majority of the litter, different habitats are created. Those under coniferous trees in constant shade will have plant and moss species not likely to be found under deciduous trees. Likewise, the animals present will differ as well.

The question for the gardener is whether to allow this litter to accumulate or to constantly clean it up. If you are not too fastidious or if your garden is large enough, you can create a litter zone, an area perhaps delineated with a log boundary or a curb, beyond which you allow natural litter to accumulate.

To enhance a litter zone, particularly for salamanders, add a few additional log chunks or blocks of decaying wood. A light hosing in dry weather, just to keep this environment damp, is also beneficial.

Wildlife Value of Composts

Depending on their shape and form, composts present a number of benefits to many garden species. One of the byproducts of the decomposition process is the release of heat. Grass clippings can be a graphic example of this. When a mound of clippings is examined a week or so after dumping you can actually see steam rising from it. Animals such as snakes and lizards enjoy this warmth. They have been known to lay their eggs in compost piles, where they are incubated by the heat generated in the pile.

A simple compost maintained as a loose pile of organic refuse is a bonus for scratching birds, especially towhees, fox sparrows and robins, which find the surface and loose edges to be first-class foraging sites.

Red Wiggler Worms

A strong colony of red wigglers will reduce most organic waste in a surprisingly short time. The benefits to the wildlife gardener include the production of a rich humus soil and a food source for worm-eating animals such as robins, shrews and moles. Check with your community recycling program for information on composting and red wiggler sources.

A big drawback to loose composting is that it often attracts unwanted rodents. A ½-inch (1-cm) screen can keep them at bay but it also excludes most birds. Salamanders, lizards and the smaller snakes can squeeze through the mesh but vertical walls are an additional barrier.

Rock Walls and Embankments

Old-fashioned rock walls, constructed from fieldstone, have largely been replaced with barbed wire or mesh fences where artificial divisions of property are desired. However, a well-constructed rock wall is more pleasing to the eye and more wildlife-friendly. Snakes, lizards, salamanders, as well as a multitude of fascinating and sometimes noisy insects, will hide or hibernate within the crevices and cavities of a rock wall.

A well-built and slightly inclined wall will last a long time. A good ratio for the incline is one to six (for every six measures high, the wall leans one measure inward from vertical). If only round, stream-tumbled rocks are available, you may need to increase the inclination to achieve the proper balance and support. A few well-placed dollops of cement can give additional stability. Spaces and cavities behind the wall, some partially filled with soft earth or sand, will increase the likelihood of winter or dry season use.

Insecticides and Herbicides

At one time or another, infuriated by weed or insect pests, every gardener feels the urge to do something about them. Often the quickest and easiest solution is to spray them with chemicals, probably one of the commonly used broadcast herbicides or pesticides. But even when applied in the most careful and diligent manner possible, under ideal conditions, the effect often goes far beyond our original intent. The well-documented effects of DDT on the populations of raptors, especially the peregrine falcon, are common knowledge. DDT and many like compounds have now turned up in bio-assays from the Antarctic.

Insecticides are particularly bad for wildlife, not because they kill the insects for which they were intended but because many of these chemicals are long-lived, remaining in the environment and the food chain. Here they persist, sometimes building up to lethal levels for organisms higher in the food chain. Herbicides, though directed towards plants, are often poisonous to animals as well.

Often, in our haste to rid plants infected by an insect pest, we react too quickly, before any of the natural controls have a chance to do their work. This was brought home recently when good friends were about to depart on a 12-day holiday. In the haste of preparations before departure one of their last observations, as they were stepping out the door, was that their tomato plants were infected by white fly. They were not able to do anything at the time, but when they arrived home, they had a pleasant surprise—their tomatoes were healthy and fit and the white fly menace had vanished. Nature had come to the rescue with a natural remedy. Granted, cures do not always occur in this manner, but they might be much more common if we had the patience to give them a chance.

Environment-Friendly Treatments

Two insecticides that appear fairly safe to vertebrates are pyrethrum and rotenone. Neither of these accumulates in the environment or enters the food chain. While manufacturers may insist that other potent chemicals are harmless if applied correctly, common sense dictates that these should only be applied in your garden as a last resort. Always consult a licensed professional before the application of any pesticide or herbicide agent.

Alternatives to these harsh treatments are available. A number of organizations distribute information on safe ways to deal with pests. Ask the manager or owner of your local nursery. Remember—pest control is a multimillion-dollar industry where the quickest solution is not necessarily the easiest or best one.

Pruning Plants to Improve Wildlife Values

The objective of pruning is to modify the growth of a plant to accentuate its beauty and usefulness or to increase its flower or fruit production. Pruning is necessary to remove unwanted, dead or diseased growth or to keep the plant to a desired form.

When thinking of pruning a tree or shrub to improve its use by wildlife, these objectives vary. In addition to improving fruit or flower production, pruning can be planned to provide better shelter or potential nesting sites.

Before pruning any plant you will need to know how it grows, particularly its season of flowering or fruiting and whether these occur on old growth or new growth. For these and other reasons, pruning is both a skill and an art.

Generally there are two types of pruning: thinning, which removes entire branches and stems to open up the form of the plant, and cutting back, in which the smaller side branches and tips of branches are removed to reduce a plant's size. This latter process produces bushier plants and is most often used with hedging. Most garden plants are pruned to open them up, but when gardening for wildlife, consider developing some areas with dense foliage. Thicker tangles are important for cover and nest sites for some sparrows, finches, robins, cardinals and waxwings.

Deadheading, the removal of dead and fading flowers, will extend the blooming period for many flowering plants, such as fuchsias, zinnias and the like, which are attractive to hummingbirds, butterflies and bees.

Thinning to reduce bulk   Shaping to achieve desired form

Acquiring Plants for the Wildlife Garden

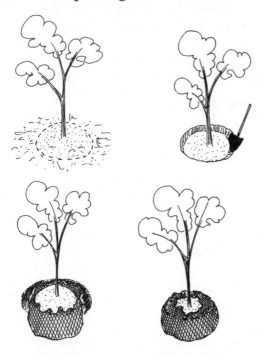

Very few nurseries specialize in plants for the wildlife garden. Most will carry a small number of good specimens, but the nursery staff may well be able to provide suggestions about acquiring others. Tell your nursery manager what you are trying to do and what you are looking for, and do not be afraid to ask for their recommendations.

Neighbors and friends may have gardens with attractive plants that they are willing to share. Some plants can be divided, others can be propagated through cuttings, layering and seed germination.

Steps in digging larger plants for transplanting. (Wire mesh holds dirt and roots together)

Layering is one of the simplest methods. It works well on shrubby plants with flexible branches that root easily. Bend a low branch to the ground, cover it with loose soil and hold it in place with a good-sized rock. Once rooted (which may take four to six months) the branch can be severed from the parent plant and moved to your garden. Gooseberries and currants are easy to propagate this way.

Many perennials not only can be divided, but also benefit from this process. Methods vary depending on the root system, but in all cases the plant is dug up and partitioned. Each piece will produce a healthy new plant.

Cuttings can often be induced to root by dipping the cut surface in a rooting compound and planting them in a mixture of peat, sand and perlite. Many garden books describe these and other propagation techniques in detail.

Transplanting is often the best method of bringing native trees, shrubs and flowers into your garden. Moving them in early spring or late fall when ground moisture and humidity are high has the best chance of success. Moving large specimens with well-established root systems can be difficult. The illustration, previous page, suggests one method by which this may be done.

Observing and Keeping Records

While great naturalists such as Charles Darwin and Henri Fabre used their gardens extensively as laboratories and kept volumes of notes on their experiments and observations, as happy amateurs we need not be so diligent. However, regularly recorded observations become an important diary of our results and achievements.

Such information, when gathered first-hand in a systematic fashion, has a number of useful purposes. These notes could form the basis for a simple list of the wildlife that visits your garden. They could become a data bank of information to assist you with further modifications and improvements. Good data may also help other gardeners or biologists document the yearly cycle or life history of a particular animal. Whatever the reason, keeping regular notes will sharpen your awareness and improve your powers of observation.

When recording observations about insects, birds, reptiles, amphibians and mammals, make sure you write down the name, time and date where you saw it and what you observed it to be doing (the who, when, where and what). This data provides valuable insights into natural history and will help you produce better results in your garden.

About Lists

While some people would call it a craze, the practice of listing by some naturalists, particularly bird watchers, can be a challenging experience. These lists may be a life list, a year list, a state or provincial list, or a backyard list. No matter what the type, they provide a simple record of species seen and identified within a given time frame or geographic location.

What Makes a Good Notebook?

- It should have a hard cover and lined or squared (graph) paper.
- Waterproof paper is a plus.
- It should be large enough that it doesn't get lost yet small enough to fit into a pocket.

Always keep it handy!

Notes and Records of Significance

Studies of natural history in North America go back over 400 years (in the Northwest just over 200 years), yet it is surprising how little is known about many of the common types of wildlife. Even today, it is not uncommon for amateur naturalists to make observations of significance in their own backyards. Many organizations, such as museums, natural history organizations and university research programs, welcome and often rely on volunteer help, and they actively encourage backyard record-keeping.

Before you contact a museum or university, have your observations confirmed by a knowledgeable member of your local naturalist club or Audubon Society chapter. Due to the great advancements in photography, an acceptable record no longer needs to be a stuffed specimen. A good clear photo with accurate supporting documentation will suffice. If a good photo is not possible, write down a detailed description on the spot, without the aid of any reference material or a field guide. These notes should indicate time, place, size, and the distinguishing field marks you observed. Comments on behavior and type of activity the animal was engaged in can also be helpful.

Making Your Wildlife Garden "Official"

In the early 1970s the National Wildlife Federation launched a program to establish a network of mini-wildlife refuges in the backyards of its members. Certification was given to those applicants who showed evidence of substantially improving wildlife habitat. A number of other organizations and wildlife agencies have followed this lead. Certification and a weatherproof sign for erection on the property are part of these programs. Check with your local wildlife agency to find out about programs in your area.

CHAPTER 16
Protecting Your Charges and Your Property

In the days when tall television aerials were the rule, it was not uncommon for flickers, our second-largest and most abundant woodpecker, to use these lofty perches as drumming stations. The sound they created could be heard for great distances, but the quality of the picture on the television set inside left much to be desired. In frustration, an acquaintance attempted to solve this annual courtship ritual problem once and for all. Resting a small caliber rifle on the eave of his back porch, he fired skyward at the offending flicker. His aim was spot-on, but not quite on the flicker. The latter departed hurriedly as the bullet neatly clipped the bracket, causing the aerial to plummet and puncture the roof. Was this justice? I leave the answer to you.

Protection of backyard wildlife is a two-way street. First, protection for your charges is important because encouraging their presence by supplying them with many of their needs places responsibility on the provider. Second, because wildlife can cause personal frustration, damage private property or be carriers of disease, we need to be cognizant of potential problems. First and foremost, wildlife gardeners must feel safe and secure in what they undertake. Generally speaking, with a few common-sense precautions, the advantages and recreational enjoyment provided by wildlife far exceed the problems.

Protecting Your Property

Any vacant space with an easy external access can become a cozy retreat for a variety of unwanted wildlife from raccoons to mud-daubing wasps. House sparrows, violet-green swallows, starlings, bats and squirrels will all take advantage of the smallest crack or flaw in a building's exterior and turn this into a home or nursery.

While all these animals may bring considerable personal enjoyment, they may also hasten the deterioration of the building. Careful and regular inspections and prompt repair of the exterior of buildings to make them wildlife-proof can provide financial savings and eliminate worries. Feeling comfortable in the presence of wildlife is a very important consideration.

Discouraging Nuisance Animals

Invariably, during the course of wildlife gardening, situations will occur in which an animal attempts to nest or build a home in a location where they are not wanted. As most animals are creatures of habit, discouraging them is often not easy. Birds that want to nest over a doorway, woodpeckers that use a gable or shingle as a drumming station, a squirrel that insists on gnawing an entrance into an attic or any one of a number of bee species that attempt to build their nest within the walls of a residence; these are just some of the many situations to be aware of. Bats are another serious concern. Outwitting these pests may not be easy, but it can be done.

Birds Nesting in Unwanted Locations

Barn swallows and robins are notorious for building their nests just under the eaves of buildings. The nests become a problem when located directly over a doorway or window. It becomes particularly messy as the young birds are about to leave the nest.

To stop nesting at these locations before it begins, remove any potential nest supports before the nesting season arrives. If this is not feasible, place balls of crumpled newspaper in the would-be nesting space. You may wish to assist this process by erecting an appropriate nesting bracket at a nearby location.

Damage From Woodpeckers

Woodpeckers, particularly flickers, find some buildings ideal sites from which to announce their amorous intentions. Well-seasoned wood, loose shingles and even metal flashings make great drumming locations. While the noise is loud, the damage is minimal.

Should this activity indicate a cavity or hollow beneath, the site may become a nesting location and a hole will follow.

Where woodpeckers are actually chiseling holes into walls, one successful remedy is to place a bag of suet at the hole. The food offering distracts the bird from its original intention.

Damage From Squirrels and Other Mammals

Modern construction materials, including the increased use of aluminum siding, soffits and roofing, have made mammal-proofing our residences much easier. These animals are always on the lookout for easy access to a cosy, warm, dark shelter. Vertical walls are a pretty good physical barrier and if all access to the roof is eliminated, most homes will be secure.

Attics make ideal roosting areas for bats. Some may even become maternal nursery sites. Hundreds of bats can descend on a favored location. Bats are capable of squeezing through spaces the size of a dime, so ensure all entrances are completely screened.

Protecting Your Charges

Ensuring that our gardens are as safe as possible for the visiting wildlife becomes a personal responsibility. While the natural environment has a great many predator-prey relationships, few of us would wish to contribute to these deliberately or be responsible for the death of individual animals. Pets, window panes and window wells all contribute their share of garden wildlife casualties.

Without any hesitation, Public Enemy No. 1 to garden wildlife is the friendly, docile and ubiquitous neighborhood cat. While people who love wildlife have ample reason to strongly dislike this family pet, one must at the same time admire its character and biological efficiency. Everything that moves, from grasshoppers to reptiles, birds and small mammals, falls prey to a cat's predatory instincts. No matter how well we feed it, or how often we warn or discipline it, a cat can seldom resist the instinct to hunt and pounce on anything small that moves. Cats are ruthlessly efficient predators.

Understanding the magnitude of the problem cats pose to urban wildlife is not easy. Studies have concluded that house cats are the primary destroyers of chickadees in North America. It is estimated that 55% of the ailments/injuries to cottontail rabbits admitted to a local veterinary hospital were cat-inflicted. Another study concluded that the average house cat kills at least one small mammal or bird each month. A 1985 study by the Washington State Department of Wildlife found "there are at least twenty outdoor cats per block in a typical urban neighborhood." If these figures hold true for other human population centers in North America, simple arithmetic tells us domestic cats destroy hundreds of millions of wild birds, small mammals and other vertebrates each year. On the beneficial side, there is no doubt that cats take a heavy toll of introduced house mice and rats. For professional wildlife managers, however, the evidence is mounting that cats pose a concern to maintaining healthy populations of many native wildlife species.

Dealing With Cats

With the exception of simple tolerance, there are at least three clear choices a gardener can take to protect their wild visitors from cats. The first is the erection of a cat-proof fence. The second is to discourage cats if and whenever they appear. The third is to remove them.

Cat-proof fence

• The Cat-Proof Fence

Australia is the country that has perfected the technique of predator control using fences. Their dog fences, to keep dingos from penetrating sheep-grazing areas, stretch for thousands of miles. A chain-link, or similar material, fence, at least 6 feet (1.8 m) high and snug to the ground is needed. While this type of fence may also eliminate raccoons and other large terrestrial animals, it has other advantages. It can demarcate property lines and is a good support for climbing vegetation. Placing a strand of barbed wire at the top and/or bottom should be considered only in extreme circumstances. Barbed wire is dangerous in natural environments and is known to maim, even kill, a considerable number of animals.

• Cat Elimination: The 1-2-3 Method

If cats are a serious problem and you feel this situation demands attention, you may wish to try the following plan.

1. Notify your neighbors that you are developing your garden as a wildlife sanctuary. Inform them that stray cats, not necessarily theirs, are causing you concern and that should the problem continue, you intend to do something about it. Ask them to make sure their pets are kept indoors or have an identification collar.

2. Purchase, borrow or build a suitable live trap and bait it accordingly. A simple, easily constructed live trap is illustrated, next page. Suitable commercial traps are available through your local hardware or farm supply store. These come in a number of different sizes and styles. Traps can sometimes be borrowed from your local S.P.C.A., animal shelter or from some government wildlife agencies.

If you catch a cat, and you know the owners, return their pet and mention that should you trap the animal again you will turn it over to the local S.P.C.A. or animal shelter. If you do not recognize the animal, you should make the effort to find out if someone else does. If no one recognizes the cat, take it to the S.P.C.A.

3. Take retrapped animals to the S.P.C.A. This method might seem drastic, but you would be surprised how many feral and neglected house cats wander our neighborhoods. Not all cat owners accept responsibility for their pets.

This is a sad situation, but every city in North America has to put down unwanted cats by the thousands each year. In Winnipeg, Manitoba, the total was in excess of 6,000 in 1998; in Greater Vancouver it was 14,000! These figures represent one cat for about every 100 people.

• Keeping Cats Indoors

It is well documented that cats that live indoors lead longer, healthier lives than those that are allowed to roam outdoors. In some cases their longevity is more than tripled! Owners of these animals benefit from knowing that their pet is safe, avoiding the dangers of traffic, diseases, parasites, poisonings or being mauled by other animals.

A Simple Box Trap

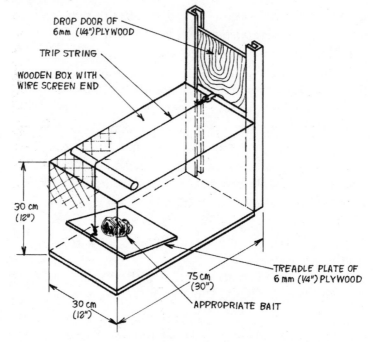

DROP DOOR OF 6mm (1/4") PLYWOOD

TRIP STRING

WOODEN BOX WITH WIRE SCREEN END

30 cm (12")

75 cm (30")

30 cm (12")

TREADLE PLATE OF 6 mm (1/4") PLYWOOD

APPROPRIATE BAIT

• Protecting Bird Feeders From Cats

To minimize the chances of cats taking birds from around feeders, the feeders must be placed at least 6½ feet (2 m) above the ground.

While it is more difficult to protect ground-feeding species like juncos and sparrows, a chicken wire or lathing screen (detailed in previous chapters, see page 102) can be used at the base of the feeding station to prevent access or ambush. A simple, free-standing portable piece of screen can also be used to block direct access routes. While these barriers may not provide complete protection, they should help minimize the problem.

• Harassing Would-Be Predators

Demonstrating your annoyance when predators enter your garden can go a long way to discouraging them. A handful of pebbles thrown, not to injure but to scare animals on the prowl, can be an effective deterrent. A soft-drink can partially filled with pebbles will make a terrific racket as it crashes and bounces after hitting the ground. This will tell most animals very plainly that their presence is not appreciated. Slingshots and catapults are not recommended as they have the potential to inflict serious injury. Once an animal has been frightened once or twice, just opening a window or a door will send it off. A good rap on a window to indicate your annoyance will also work for a time.

Where the problem and danger from cats becomes acute, the only possible remedy may be to stop feeding altogether, or only feed larger, less susceptible species such as starlings, pigeons and crows.

About Hawks and Owls

Cooper's and sharp-shinned hawks, shrikes, and in some instances, small owls, may become frequent visitors to feeding stations. In fact any area which is developed to become a mecca for wildlife will also become a magnet and preferred hunting location for their natural predators.

Attitudes towards these predators vary, but it must be remembered that all hawks and owls are protected by law and cannot be shot, trapped or harmed, except under permit. Predation by these raptors is one of the natural checks and balances that play an important role in maintaining healthy songbird populations. Avoiding predators is part of an individual's day-to-day survival, similar in a number of respects to our daily running the traffic gauntlet.

Protecting wildlife in our garden from raptors follows the same general principles as protections from cats: provide good escape routes, install large mesh to block access and use harassment to keep them at arm's length.

Hawks and owls are among the most fascinating of birds. While we may not like their food procurement methods, they are impressive to observe.

A Backyard Garden Safety Check

Architects, planners and builders are often totally unaware that the creations they design may have serious implications for wildlife. From wells to windows, just about everything built into a house or garden can have a positive or negative impact on wildlife.

- Pits, pools, curbs and window wells with perpendicular sides become traps that many small creatures can easily enter, but from which escape can be difficult or impossible. If these traps cannot be avoided in the construction of a facility, then some form of egress, such as a ladder or ramp, is required. Pools should have a similar shallow sloping portion as part of their design.

- More small birds, and many larger ones, are injured or killed by flying into windows than most of us would care to acknowledge. Estimates range in excess of 95 million birds annually! In many cases these collisions only stun the victim. When these casualties are placed in a warm, dry, quiet location (a cardboard box is ideal) these birds will often recover quickly and then can be released.

  Windows, due to reflection or another window behind, often appear as tunnels to small birds. This illusion tricks the bird into believing they can fly right through. Many solutions, some listed below, have been proposed with varying results.

- Pull the curtains to eliminate the tunnel appearance of a second window.

- Hang strips of silver paper or colored ribbon in front of the window.

- Place decals on the window to indicate the barrier. For thermal pane windows, the placing of bars between the panes during construction gives the appearance of a lattice.

- Hang a coarse netting across the face of the window.

At the Bamfield Marine Station in British Columbia, 4-inch (10-cm) fish netting was hung from the eaves, and silhouettes of Cooper's hawks were cut out and hung in the netting. Black, 1-inch-square (2.5-cm) birdnetting, mounted on a frame and placed about 1 foot (30 cm) away from the windows, has been found to reduce collision fatalities dramatically.

Where collisions between birds and windows persist or are fairly frequent, perhaps other factors are at play, such as the location of feeding stations or birdbaths. To eliminate direct flight paths, perhaps feeding stations or bathing areas should be relocated or a tree or shrub placed between these features and the window.

What to Do With Casualties

There is always a tinge of sadness when we come across small birds or mammals that have died in our gardens. Often these casualties have educational or scientific value. Place them in a clear plastic bag, labeled with the date, location and name of the person who found the specimen. Try to identify it if you can and contact your local museum, high school, college or university biology department. Often they will appreciate and have use for these specimens in their programs.

To keep these specimens is an offense in some jurisdictions, so exercise caution and seek permission before attempting to keep these for personal use.

Protecting Your Garden

Should you be a keen gardener eager to produce fruit and vegetables, encouraging birds to come to your garden could prove disastrous. Certainly you do not want to give the potential thieves an open invitation to raid your crops.

For incursions by deer and raccoons, a good fence works best. Chain link is probably the best and, for deer, it must be at least 6½ feet (2 m) high. Individual plants can be protected by a circle of lathing screen secured in place by two or three pegs driven well into the ground. For deer there are a number of repellants available that all work to a degree. None is as good as a good fence!

Window-Bashing Birds

Each spring as our neighborhood birds begin their courtship rituals leading to their nesting season, some individual males have a terrible time distinguishing between their reflections in windows and a true rival. Watching and listening to this constant bashing is very distractive and distressing. Robins, in particular, can be extremely persistent in this activity. It is not unusual for them to pursue their supposed rival for several weeks at a number of different windows.

Aside from eliminating the bird apparently bent on self destruction, here are two solutions. First, eliminate the perch or perches from which the bird can see its reflection. The second solution is to hang a large sheet of brown waterproof paper over the outside of the window to eliminate reflection. Even with these measures in place, there is some indication that once conditioned to this activity, your male bird may search out other windows to continue this activity.

A good deer fence can be designed with both vertical and/or horizontal barriers. A vertical barrier must be at least 6½ feet (2 m) high, but a 'T'-shaped fence can be lower if the width across the top of the T is at least 3 feet (1 m). Deer are reluctant to jump high and wide obstacles.

Perhaps the most effective way to keep unwanted avian guests from stealing the rewards from fruit trees and berry bushes is to cover them with birdnetting. Using this netting, available from nurseries or farm and garden outlets, is not without some risk to wildlife. Birds do occasionally get tangled in the mesh and die.

Some birds, particularly house finches, start their orchard raiding when fruit trees are still in bud. To reduce or eliminate this early damage, you may have to set your nets up early in the season.

Rats and Mice

Just as hawks and owls will visit your feeding station in hopes of picking off an

Bird window

easy meal, rats and house mice will also find your station an easy target. Though these animals are seldom seen, your efforts to provide cover and a high-energy food source play right into their hands. Rats and mice are silent foragers as a rule. Under cover of darkness they often visit unnoticed. Our native deer mouse or white-footed mouse is also a nighttime forager. If you need to bring in a vermin control program, make sure you can distinguish house mice from deer mice and voles!

Today, most unwanted creatures like rats and mice are controlled through the use of poison baits. These are indiscriminate killers. When problems arise, rather than resorting to poisons, consider live traps. These portable units permit the discriminating removal of the unwanted and the release of the desirable species. Drowning is a quick, easy and humane method of dispatching the unwanted. Live traps of the appropriate size are available through local garden supply companies.

Poisons should be used only as a very last resort. If you must use them, contact your local agricultural office for the latest information on the poisons available, the recommended dosage and the precautions that need to be followed.

You may find that in small, neatly groomed gardens where native mammals, salamanders and snakes are not likely to be present, the provision of brush piles and cavities may only encourage rats and mice. In these circumstances, these features should be eliminated.

Discouraging Unwanted Species

When developing a wildlife garden there are invariably a few surprises, things we had not counted on. Some are pleasant surprises, and then there are ones that cause frustration. Animals that are persistent and domineering fall into this latter category. These often include squirrels, jays, starlings, house sparrows and wasps.

Outwitting these pests is not easy, but it can be done. There are three general recommendations for minimizing problems.
1. Provide foods that these species do not like.
2. Provide their favored food at a second isolated location where they are less likely to be a nuisance.
3. Attempt to exclude them, harass them, or trap and relocate them.

Outwitting Squirrels

Unwanted squirrels at a feeding station are difficult to discourage. They are exceedingly clever at finding access to feeders. You can attempt to squirrel-proof a feeder or use plastic squirrel guards, which use this same concept and are commercially available.

To make this really effective, keep the feeder away from over-hanging branches and other launching pads from which the squirrel can jump. You might want to provide squirrel foods in a different location with an easy access, then squirrel-proof, as best you can, the locations where they are unwanted.

I once observed an amusing occurrence when a timid red squirrel refused to jump to a swinging bird feeder stocked with peanut pieces. The squirrel could obviously smell them but remained frustrated until a flock of chickadees came along and started carting away the kernels for storage. As the chickadees got lazier and these flights

101 Ways to Outwit a Squirrel

Outwitting squirrels can be a real challenge—so much so that there is a 300-page book by Bill Adler: *Outwitting Squirrels— 101 Cunning Stratagems.* There are more ideas (and chuckles) here than you could ever need.

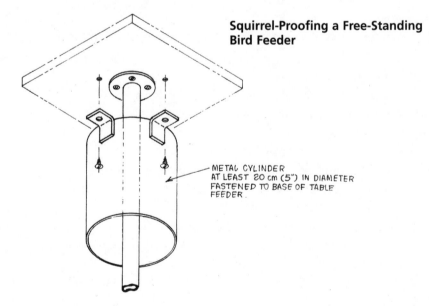

Squirrel-Proofing a Free-Standing Bird Feeder

METAL CYLINDER AT LEAST 20 cm (5") IN DIAMETER FASTENED TO BASE OF TABLE FEEDER.

became shorter, crevices in the bark of the tree where the feeder was located became the birds' repositories. This worked out well for the squirrel. The chickadees were now working for the squirrel who was afraid to jump!

Outwitting Jays

Both the eastern blue jay and the western Steller's jay are noted hoarders. Both are lovely, colorful, somewhat raucous birds that have a propensity for carrying away more groceries than they could ever eat. These they store for lean times, but even with a bird feeder as a year-round source, they never seem to lose this habit. With unshelled peanuts, one is never enough. Using their gular pouch, they can carry away two, sometimes even three, peanuts at a time.

You can discourage this activity by barring access to the feeders with a sheath of lathing screen that allows small birds to get through. To keep jays coming back, put out only a few peanuts each day. My father had great fun with this. He would toss out four or five peanuts, then whistle loudly. Sure enough, in a very short while the jays would arrive.

Discouraging Starlings

Starlings are highly mobile and virtually omnivorous. Around food sources they tend to be gregarious and aggressive. They also prefer open areas. Due to their size, screening them away from feeders is a marginal possibility. Starlings tend to be skittish and can be frightened easily. If you persist, they can be kept at bay. Starlings are not normally seed eaters, and they find the smaller seeds and sunflower seeds difficult to handle and not particularly attractive. Another tactic is to stop your feeding program for a week. With luck they will move on to another area.

Starlings build large bulky nests in cavities and nest boxes that are fairly deep. They need a fairly large entrance more than 2 inches (5 cm) in diameter. While they can squeeze through smaller openings, cramped entrances and chambers are not to their liking. To discourage starlings keep your nest boxes small, with entrances less than 1½ inches (4 cm) and relatively close above the floor.

Discouraging House Sparrows

As well as being able to tolerate humans in large doses, house sparrows adapt readily to new situations. These attributes, combined with their size and food preferences, make them difficult to outwit at feeding stations.

As nesting competitors to violet-green swallows, they are particularly bothersome at nest boxes. Modifying the hole (see illustration, page 84) has been demonstrated to be highly favorable to swallows and an effective deterrent to sparrows.

Eliminating Wasps

Wasps often become serious pests around hummingbird feeders. However, their quarrelsome nature allows us to keep their numbers in check. Place a shallow pan of water (a garbage pail lid is a good size) under the feeder, and the quarrelling wasps will fall into the pan and quickly drown. A drop or two of liquid detergent hastens the drowning. If you count the casualties, you will have an even number just about every time, as both combatants die side-by-side.

A simple funnel trap, baited with a piece of fish or moist dog food, will trap hundreds of wasps in a relatively short time. A similar type

A Simple Funnel Trap for Wasps

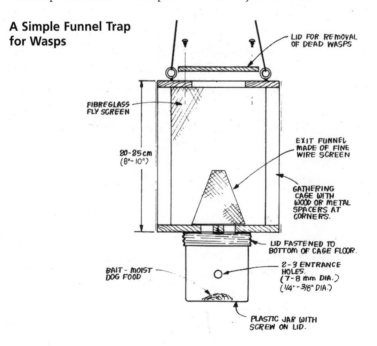

LID FOR REMOVAL OF DEAD WASPS

FIBREGLASS FLY SCREEN

20-25 cm (8"-10")

EXIT FUNNEL MADE OF FINE WIRE SCREEN

GATHERING CAGE WITH WOOD OR METAL SPACERS AT CORNERS.

LID FASTENED TO BOTTOM OF CAGE FLOOR.

BAIT - MOIST DOG FOOD

2-3 ENTRANCE HOLES. (7-8 mm DIA.) (1/4"-3/8" DIA.)

PLASTIC JAR WITH SCREW ON LID.

of trap is available from hardware stores. The secret is to place traps out early in the season, preventing the population from increasing exponentially.

Eliminating Mosquitoes From Garden Pools

Although mosquitoes have a fascinating life cycle (see page 35), they are certainly not desirable in garden pools. In most pools that have established a balance with healthy populations of aquatic insects, such as water beetles and dragonflies, mosquitoes will not be a problem. If mosquitoes are a problem add a few goldfish. In southern areas, where waters remain fairly warm all year, gambusia, or mosquitofish, will make short work of any larvae.

Protection—A Concluding Word

The solutions and ideas put forward here cover only a few of the major problems relating to the gardener's desire to have wildlife nearby. Some of the solutions suggested may appear to be a little drastic, but just as oil and water do not mix, many elements of wildlife gardening can be incompatible as well. Finding good and practical solutions that avoid confrontation requires trial and error, patience, discussion and communication. It is always nice to learn about creative solutions to these and other problems.

CHAPTER 17
Backyard First Aid—Caring for Sick or Injured Animals

Prepared by Liz Thunstrom,
Wildlife Rescue Association of British Columbia

Everyone with a garden will be faced, at one time or another, with the dilemma of a sick, injured or orphaned wild creature. At such times, it takes a stout heart and a clear head to put reality before emotion. Does this animal really need human help? People, especially those with children, will be presented with casualties and expected to perform miracles for this new "instant pet."

Each year in spring and early summer, wildlife problems increase. This is the time young animals are born and start to grow up and parents are fully engaged in providing food and shelter for their offspring. Wildlife rehabilitation facilities, the Society for Prevention of Cruelty to Animals, veterinary clinics and government agencies are swamped with calls on what to do with apparently orphaned babies, birds attacking windows and stove pipes or nesting in unwanted or unsafe places, injuries from cats and cars, and many others. Many of these animals do not need our help. Others, despite our efforts, are too badly injured to survive even with the very best of care.

Sometimes, however, it is possible to save an injured animal if some simple, easy basic practices are followed. One of the best ways to increase chances for survival is to simply provide a secure hiding place that minimizes the animal's fear and shock, while qualified help is being contacted.

It must be stressed that if wild creatures are to recover fully for release back into the wild, they must receive prompt specialized care. It is pointless to hand-raise a baby, for example, when in the end it will never be able to survive in the wild.

Are They Really Orphaned?

When a young bird or mammal is found alone, it is easy to jump to the conclusion that it must be lost, orphaned or abandoned. In reality, this is seldom the case. The mother may be off finding food, the youngster may have wandered or hopped away from cover, or it may have strayed from its nest or den. The bond between parents and their young is exceedingly strong; be assured that parents will usually return to their young. Wild babies always do better with their own parents!

Birds

Baby birds frequently fall, hop or are pushed from their nests. If you can locate the nest, the best action is to put them back. Despite popular belief, birds will not reject babies that have been handled by humans—our birds have no sense of smell.

Nestlings

- are not feathered, their eyes may be closed
- are not able to stand or perch
- beaks open directly upwards
- have large yellow corners to their beaks known as gape flanges
- are not able to regulate their own body temperature.

These birds belong in their nests. If you cannot reach the nest, make a substitute from a berry basket or hanging planter lined with paper towels or moss and place it as high up and as close to the nest

How to Tell if Help Is Needed—A Check List

- How long has the animal been alone? Is it an hour or overnight?
- What is the animal's condition? Cold? Wet? Thin?
- What are the weather conditions?
- Is the animal obviously injured—wing hanging, visible blood, maggots?
- Is it lying in feces?
- Is the animal in immediate danger?
- Is there a dead adult or sibling nearby?
- Have you watched for an hour or more for signs of an adult?

Only when the answer to most of these questions is a definite YES does the animal need your assistance to survive.

as possible. This "nest" should be sheltered from the sun and rain. Do not attempt to feed the babies, but watch from a good distance for an hour or two to see if the parents carry out their duties at this new location. The hunger calls from the young will attract the parents. If there is no sign of the adults after two hours, the nestling will need assistance.

Fledglings
• are partially or fully feathered
• are able to stand and perch but cannot fly
• have their eyes open and can follow movements
• have less obvious gape flanges
• can regulate their body temperature
• are active and will begin to leave their nest on their own
• still need to be fed by their parents

Once fully feathered, young birds leave the nest and do not return to it. They cannot fly well. Developing the strength to fly takes from a few hours for robins and starlings to a week or more for fledgling crows. At this stage the youngsters sit in low shrubbery or on the ground waiting for the parents to bring them food. The time between feedings gradually increases as the young birds begin to follow their parents. This exercise strengthens wing, breast and leg muscles. This is also the time when they learn to find their own food.

If you see parents nearby, leave the youngster alone but keep the area safe from predators, especially cats. Do not become a bird napper! If the parent is not visible, gently put the baby onto a low branch in the same area. Should the adults not return after two hours, the youngster may need assistance.

Young birds are especially vulnerable to cats. Urban cats are found in higher concentrations than any natural predators.

Mammals
Mammals like squirrels, raccoons, rabbits and deer leave their young safely hidden while they forage for food, until the babies are strong enough to follow. Usually these youngsters lie quietly for

extended periods of time. Doe rabbits only return to feed their young twice a day.

Never approach baby mammals closely; observe them from a distance. Mammals, unlike birds, have a keen sense of smell. Handling young imparts the human scent that disturbs the mother and is detectable to predators. (Newborn mammals have no smell, making them difficult for predators to find.) If the baby appears in good condition, leave it overnight, giving the mother the opportunity to return. If there is no sign of the mother the next morning, use the checklist outlined at the beginning of this chapter.

Here is a suggestion for an easy way to see if a rabbit is returning to her babies. Place a long piece of grass across the nest or runway. If it has been disturbed, you will know the adult has been home.

Emergency Care and First Aid

Once you have decided that an animal needs assistance, it is important to remember Hippocrates' words "do no harm." Stress and shock are the biggest killers of injured wildlife. Remember, your patient views you as a predator, not a friend. Being petted, handled or talked to is terrifying for it. Always keep your own safety in mind as well. Hurt and frightened animals will use their last strength in an attempt to get free.

Young Birds

Place your patients in a temporary nest from folded tissue in a berry basket and place this inside a ventilated box or ice cream bucket. Provide a source of heat (the top of a fridge is good) and keep away from drafts.

If the babies are alert and gaping (begging for food), you can prepare a simple emergency diet (see page 168) and offer a small amount on a toothpick or stir-stick, placing the mixture as far back in their mouths as possible. Feed every twenty minutes, throughout the day. Keep the

Shock

Shock is a general term for the profound depression of vital processes associated with reduced blood volume and pressure often caused by severe injury. In wild animals the treatment for shock is to keep the injured animal warm, quiet and undisturbed in a dark enclosure. Animals in shock should not be given food or water. Specialized care is required.

food off faces and feathers and the nest clean of droppings. Very young birds produce poop tidily in a mucus sac, making cleanup easy.

Orphaned ducklings and goslings need to be kept dry. A cardboard box, lined with layers of paper towels and covered with a sheet or towel, works well. These birds are able to eat on their own. They need soaked chick starter (available from farm supply outlets) placed in a small, stable dish. They also need a constant supply of water dispensed in such a manner that the little ones cannot get their down soiled. Placing a bottle in the middle of the water dish will allow drinking only. Goslings are easily adopted out to another goose family. This should be done as soon as possible.

Young Mammals

These little fellows need warmth and darkness. A nest made from an old wool sock or toque, placed in a cardboard box next to a source of warmth, is ideal. The babies should be covered, but be able to move short distances away from the heat source.

Always allow these animals to warm up before attempting to feed them. Never feed them cow's milk or human baby formula, as this is indigestible and causes life-threatening diarrhea. Never give anything to an animal that is unconscious.

If you cannot get the patient to a rehabilitator within 24 hours, you can offer them rehydrating solution or Pedialyte, available at drugstores. Use a small pet nurser, eyedropper or 1-cc plastic diabetic syringe. Warm this liquid to body temperature and feed slowly and carefully, with the baby lying on its stomach on a towel. If fluid is inhaled into the lungs, it will cause pneumonia. Feed every four hours, around the clock. This formula also provides energy. Following feeding, the genital area must be wiped with a soft tissue to encourage defecation. In nature, mother licks them clean.

All baby mammals must have special milk formulas to grow properly. It is essential that they get qualified care as quickly as possible. Youngsters with their eyes open can be offered small portions of their appropriate foods. Never feed them bread or other human foods.

Rabbits must be left alone as much as possible. Feed them only every six to seven hours. If their eyes are open, they do not need to be hand-fed—they will nibble on greens and apple on their own. Opossums are very different. If they are still in their mother's pouch and their eyes are closed, they are unable to suckle on their own and require immediate specialized care for survival.

Baby mammals are extremely cute but grow up quickly and are never truly tame. Always keep the true needs of the animal in mind. Children need to learn the right way to interact with nature and that young wild animals are not to be considered as play-things. Edwin Way Teal in *Circle of the Seasons* wrote, "Those who wish to pet and baby wild animals, love them. But those who respect their natures and wish to let them live normal lives, love them more."

Injured Adults

Injuries of all types, especially those caused by cats, require imme-diate medical attention. The number-one problem is not the injury itself, but shock.

Wild animals, injured and cornered, bite and scratch aggressive-ly. Consider your own safety first. Here are some suggestions:

• Always wear heavy gloves.

• Drop a towel, jacket or blanket completely over the animal. Once the animal's head and eyes are covered, it will become quieter and easier to handle.

• Gently place the animal in a stout cardboard box or suitable con-tainer with adequate ventilation. Cover securely and place it in a warm, dark location.

• Keep the animal quiet and free from disturbance, particularly pets and small children.

• Do not offer it food, water or brandy!

Once the patient is warm and secure, locate the nearest experi-enced help. The local S.P.C.A., humane society, veterinarian, wildlife rehabilitation center, wildlife or conservation authority should be able to offer the assistance required or advise where to get it. The treatment of wild animals is often different from that given domestic or companion animals. The sooner treatment is started, the better are the chances of the animal making a full recovery.

If immediate help is not available, the following emergency measure may be helpful. After 15 to 20 minutes, quietly open the box and assess the inmate. Do this in an enclosed room, with windows covered and toilet seats down. Keeping its head covered, check the animal.

• Is it alert and up on its feet or is it comatose or lethargic?

• Is it convulsing?

• Are limbs or wings at odd angles?

• Is there any sign of blood?

If the creature is conscious but groggy, it is probably in shock. Keep the animal in its container, administer rehydrating solution and repeat this operation every 20 minutes for one or two hours. Once the animal seems alert, offer small amounts of appropriate foods (not bread) and some rehydrating solution in a small, low container like a jar lid. (Large dishes can spill or spoil, or the animal may sit in them.) Continue to seek professional help.

Following are some common injuries.

• Birds, because of their specialized anatomy with hollow bones and airsacs, develop severe infections more rapidly than mammals. Scratches and puncture marks from a cat's claws and teeth infect very rapidly. A course of antibiotics is required for survival. If immediate help is not available, keep the creature's head covered and gently clean small wounds with a mild saline solution before applying an antibiotic ointment sparingly. Severe wounds, especially to the head and abdomen, are life-threatening and require medical help.

• Bones poking through the skin and situations with extensive bleeding need to be attended to by a vet. Keep the animal quiet and warm but do not attempt to treat the injury yourself.

• If you suspect poisoning, try to ascertain the type of poison and call the nearest poison control center for help.

- Birds often injure themselves by flying into windows. If a bird is stunned, pick it up to avoid predators finding it and give it the warm, dark quiet treatment. Leave it alone for an hour or two in a small enclosed room, such as a bathroom. After this period, see if the bird can fly. Most often it will only be stunned and after a short period of rest is ready for release. Birds found after 5 P.M. can be kept overnight. If the bird is unable to fly, its wings are drooping or it seems lethargic, contact a wildlife professional for further advice.

See Chapter 16, pages 152–154 for ideas on how to prevent birds from becoming window casualties.

Injured Bats

It is not advisable to care for injured bats at home, and you should never handle bats with bare hands. If you find one on the ground during the day, scoop it up with a dust pan and move it to a near-by tree where the bat can await nightfall. For bats to become air-borne they need to be elevated. Placing it in a tree will allow it to climb to a suitable height.

Injured Deer

These animals are extremely nervous and difficult to handle. Often they are tranquilized before treatment. During transportation they need to be blindfolded and securely wrapped in a tarp or blanket to immobilize their sharp hooves. Injured deer will need veterinary care.

Injured Reptiles

Give injured snakes and turtles basic care for shock. Open wounds can be cleaned and treated with antiseptic ointment, but these heal more slowly than the wounds of birds or mammals. An old aquarium with a tight-fitting lid of fly screen makes

Dehydrating Solution

To 1 cup (250 mL) of warm water add 1 teaspoon (5 mL) of sugar and ⅛ teaspoon (.5 mL) of salt. Mix until all the solids are dissolved.

With an eyedropper or syringe, place a drop on the tip of the bird's beak or the side of the mammal's mouth. This solution is sticky, so be careful to keep it off feathers and fur. Notice if the animal swallows. Never try to feed an unconscious animal.

an ideal sick bay. A turtle that has swallowed a fish hook or has a damaged shell will need veterinary care.

Release these animals as soon as possible in the area where they were first found.

Injured Amphibians

Frogs, toads and newts occasionally require first aid for injuries and broken limbs. They increasingly fall afoul of weed cutters being used to trim long grass in moist areas and around garden pools. Keep the injured animal on damp moss in a covered aquarium. Small abrasions can be treated with antiseptic ointment. Broken limbs will often heal on their own.

These animals eat only live insects, which can be released into their enclosure.

Emergency Diets

Human foods such as bread, processed cereals, potato chips and hamburger are not healthy for wild animals. Once you have identified the injured animal, look for general references that will tell you the natural food the animal eats. Here are some examples.

• Sparrows and birds with heavy strong beaks. Try budgie seed.

• Robins, thrushes, jays and crows. Try the emergency diet (left) or seasonal fruits such as berries, sliced grapes and small pieces of apple.

• Warblers, chickadees and wrens— birds with small, fine beaks. Try small insects like aphids, crane flies and fruit flies. Many pet shops sell meal worms if you cannot find enough insects in your garden.

• Ducks. Try duck pellets, grains, lettuce and grass.

Emergency Bird Food Diet

• Hard-boiled egg yolk
• Dog or cat chow

Soak the pet chow in water to soften it to the consistency of soft butter and blend in the mashed egg yolk.

Growing birds require a balanced diet to remain healthy. Inadequate diets cause rickets and stunting of growth and feather development. The above diet is adequate for about 24 hours, after which help from a licensed rehabilitator is required.

- Herons and kingfishers. May accept bait fish, live goldfish or minnows in a pan of water.

- Raptors and birds of prey. Require live or dead mice (never feed them hamburger as it is too fatty for them to digest).

These foods do not constitute a natural diet and should be used in the short term only. Severe diet deficiencies can cause blindness, rickets, stunted feather growth and even paralysis in young animals. Every year numerous wild animals die in captivity due to improper diets. Deformed and unhealthy animals can never be released back into the wild.

Disease and Wildlife

If you encourage wildlife onto your property, or attempt to care for animals in your home, it is important to be aware that a number of diseases and parasites can be transmitted from wild animals to humans and pets. The variety is considerable, but as with most concerns, the chances of contracting these can be greatly reduced by some very simple precautions.

Always wear gloves, latex or leather, when handling wild animals and always wash your hands thoroughly even after gardening. Pets and caged birds should be kept well away from wildlife whenever possibly as a precaution. Children should be discouraged from handling captive wild animals—their good intentions can create additional stress.

If you are bitten, cleanse the wound well with antiseptic, and report to your family doctor or nearest health unit. If rabies is suspected, the animal will be needed for testing.

Signs of Disease

Any wild animal acting in an unusual manner should be approached carefully and handled with extreme caution. Better still, stay clear and report the animal to local health authorities. If the animal appears disoriented, unusually tame, or highly aggressive, these may be symptoms of rabies. Squirrels, skunks, raccoons and bats may be carriers. Rabies is transmitted in the saliva of the infected animal. Gloves used to handle the animal should be destroyed after use.

To Keep or Not to Keep

The temptation to keep found, orphaned or injured wildlife is indeed strong. It is also illegal without a permit in many jurisdictions. Penalties can be quite severe. Whatever the circumstances, those who take wildlife into their possession should quickly determine what the regulations are for their area and act accordingly.

If you are sincerely concerned about a wild animal's well-being, have it attended to by a professional to increase its chances for survival. Wild animals also need contact with their own species and require specialized and demanding care if they are eventually to be released into a natural environment.

The Bottom Line

In this chapter some very basic guidelines are put forward to help the gardener cope with wildlife emergencies. Sometimes, however, the kindest thing we can give an injured creature is a humane release from its suffering.

Nothing, however, takes the place of common sense. If you act promptly, with the animal's best interest at heart, the patient may eventually be returned to its natural environment and live out its normal life as well as give pleasure to nature lovers. One injured robin brought into Wildlife Rescue continued to return for five years after its release.

Children can gain valuable insights by watching a mother bird encourage her offspring to take off with her. One youngster of my acquaintance spent a whole afternoon lying under a garden hedge with his squirt gun to keep cats away. His reward, still remembered years later, was seeing a family of young starlings gain the fence, then follow their mother to the rooftop.

Wild creatures never look back. When offered their freedom they are gone, back to their own world where they belong. As wildlife gardeners, we can both help them along their way and enjoy many happy hours of entertainment in the process.

SELECTED REFERENCES

Since *Attracting Backyard Wildlife* first appeared more than ten years ago, the number of books, articles and general information about wildlife gardening has expanded incredibly. The following is a sampler of some popular references that should be helpful. Your local library service should have most of these on their shelves. Many nurseries will have a selection of suitable titles as well, particularly those in the "Gardening series" category.

Gardening Series

Sunset Gardening Series by the editorial staff of Sunset Book and *Sunset* magazine. Menlo Park, CA: Sunset Publishing Corporation.
The Western Garden Book, 1961. (An incredible reference—also contains information on butterfly and hummingbird gardening)
Ideas for Small Space Gardens by Kathryn L. Arthurs.
Garden Pools, Fountains and Waterfalls, 1992.
Water Gardens, senior editors Jim McRae and Pierre Horce-Douglas, 1997.
Gardening in Containers, 1967.

Ortho Book Library Series, St. Louis, MO: Ortho Books.
How to Attract Birds by Michael McKinley, 1999.
How to Attract Hummingbirds and Butterflies by John V. Dennis, Cedric Crocker, Nancy Arbuckle and Matthew Tekulsky, 1991.
Garden Pools and Fountains by Edward B. Clafin, 1988.
Environmentally Friendly Gardening by Jeff Ball, 1992.

Stokes Backyard Nature Book Series by Donald and Lillian Stokes. Boston: Little Brown & Co.
Bird Gardening Book, 1998.
Butterfly Book, 1991.
Hummingbird Book, 1989.
Purple Martin Book, 1997.

Rodale Press, Emmaus, PA.
Your Backyard Wildlife Garden by M. Schneck. 1992.
Gardening for Wildlife by C. Tufts and P. Loewer, 1995.

Butterfly Gardening

The Butterfly Garden by Mathew Tekulsky. Boston:
The Harvard Common Press, 1985.

The Audubon Society Handbook for Butterfly Watchers by R.M. Pyle.
New York: Charles Scribner's Sons, 1984.

Butterfly Gardening: Creating Summer Magic in Your Gardens by the
Xerces Society/Smithsonian Institute. San Francisco:
Sierra Club Books, 1980.

Insect-Friendly Gardens

Rodale's Color Handbook of Garden Insects by Anna Carr. Emmaus, PA:
Rodale Press, 1979.

Peterson Field Guide Series: A Field Guide to the Insects by D.J. Borror and
R.E. White. Boston: Houghton Mifflin Company, 1970.

Golden Guide Series: Spiders and their Kin by H.W. Levi and L.R. Levi.
New York: Golden Books, 1997.

Water Gardening

*Golden Guide Series: Pondlife - a Guide to Common Plants and Animals
of North American Ponds and Lakes* by G.K. Reid et al. New York:
Golden Books.

Sunset Gardening Book Series: Water Gardens. Menlo Park, CA:
Sunset Books, 1997.

Amphibians

Amphibians of North America: A Guide to Field Identification by H.M. Smith.
New York: Golden Press, 1978.

Amphibians of Oregon, Washington and British Columbia by C.C. Corkran
and C. Thoms. Edmonton: Lone Pine Publishing, 1996.

Reptiles

*Peterson Field Guide Series: A Field Guide to the Reptiles and Amphibians
of Eastern and Central North America* by R. Conant. Boston:
Houghton Mifflin, 1975.

*Peterson Field Guide Series: A Field Guide to the Western Reptiles and
Amphibians* by R.C. Stebbins. Boston: Houghton Mifflin, 1985.

Mammals

Mammals of North America: Temperate and Arctic Regions by A. Forsythe. Willowdale, ON: Firefly Books, 1999.

America's Neighborhood Bats: Understanding and Learning to Live in Harmony With Them by M.D. Tuttle (Bat Conservation International). Austin: University of Texas Press.

The Bat House Builder's Handbook by M.D. Tuttle and D.M. Hensley. Austin: University of Texas Press, 1999.

Birds

Many excellent North American field guides are available. Consult your local library or book store for a guide to the birds of your city, state or province.

The Audubon Society Guide to Attracting Birds by S.W. Kress. New York: Charles Scribner's Sons, 1985.

The Audubon Bird Feeder Handbook: the Complete Guide to Feeding and Observing Birds by R. Burton. New York: Charles Scribner's Sons, 1995.

The Complete Guide to Bird Feeding by J.V. Dennis. New York: Alfred A. Knopf, 1975.

Balcony and Patio Gardening

Ideas for Small Space Gardens. Menlo Park, CA: Sunset Books, 1978.

Container Gardening. Menlo Park, CA: Sunset Books, 1998.

Garden Planning

Planning Your Garden by A. de Verteuil and V. Burton. North Vancouver: Whitecap Books, 1988.

Landscaping for Wildlife in the Pacific Northwest by R. Link. Seattle: University of Washington Press, 1999.

Gardening

The Wildlife Gardener by J.V. Dennis. New York: Alfred A. Knopf, 1999.

Protection

Protecting your Garden from Animal Damage. St. Louis, MO: Ortho Books, 1994.

INDEX

A

Admiral, 13
Air conditioner, 96, 120
Alder, 11
Allen's hummingbird, 74
Amphibians, 44-51, 53; gardens for,
51-52; injured, 168
Anglewing, 12, 13, 19
Anise swallowtail, 11
Anna's hummingbird, 72, 73, 74 77, 80
Antennae, 15, 25; distinction, butterfly,
skipper, moths, 14; long-horned
beetle, 26; moths, 18
Anting, 98
Ants, 26, 27, 53, 73, 78, 98;
carpenter, 59
Aphids, 22, 26, 168
Apple, 13, 88, 101, 129, 130, 133
Aquatic bugs, 33
Aquatic salamanders, 48 (See also
Salamanders)
Aquatic plants (See Plants suitable for
pools)
Arbutus, 104
Arrowhead, 43
Artificial underground burrow, 62
Aspen, 19
Asters, 16, 29
Audubon Society, 7, 17, 144
Avenues of view, 128

B

Bachelor buttons, 16
Bait: butterfly or moth, 18; crayfish, 34;
mice, 63; poison, 155
Balconies: gardening for, 117-122;
plants for, 118
Balsam, 106
Barn swallows, 82, 85, 86, 87, 146
Barren areas: hardy trees and shrubs
with wildlife values, 135; plants for
quick cover, 134; solutions for, 133;
trees and shrubs for northern
locations, 136
Bats, 60, 147, 148; big brown, 68-69;
injured, 167; little brown, 68-69
Bee balm, 75
Bees, 26-28, 73, 78, 132; as social
insects, 27; bumblebees, 27;

Bees (cont.)
honey bees, 27; leafcutting bee, 27;
orchard or mason bee, 27
Beetles, 23, 25: ground beetle, 25;
ladybird beetle, 25; long-horned
beetle, 25; scarab beetle, 25; water
beetle, 33
Birch, 15, 73, 87, 104
Bird feeders, 103, 121; cleaning, 108;
hopper, 103, 112; keeping food dry,
107; locating, 113; platform, 107;
pole, 122; protecting bird feeders
from cats, 150; selective, 113; tray,
112; types of, 112
Bird food: bread and kitchen scraps,
112; chick scratch, 109; common
bird foods, 109-112; cone feeder,
116; emergency bird food diet, 168;
fledglings, 161; food preferences of
downtown birds, 121; keeping dry,
107; millet, 110; nesting in unwanted
locations, 147; nestlings, 161;
niger seed, 110; peanut butter,
peanut hearts, peanuts, 111; suet,
111; sugar water for house finches,
121; sunflower seeds, 110; whole
wheat, 110; winter bird food
preferences, 108-109; winter bird
food recipes, 115-116
Bird territories, 88
Birdbaths, 40, 95-98; adding noise, 96;
for small mammals, 70; lawn
sprinklers, 97; water from an air
conditioner, 96; winter, 116
Birders, 82, 90, 92, 102, 105
Birdhouses, 82-87; annual maintenance,
86; nest box measurements, 83
Birds: anting, 98; Breeding Bird Count,
90; Christmas Bird Count, 106;
common garden, 89; dust baths,
97; feeding summer birds, 98-99;
keeping food dry, 107; injured, 160,
161-164, 168; locating your feeder,
113; migration, 102; nesting, 82-85;
preening, 99; providing nesting
materials, 90; providing water in
winter, 116; seed- and fruit-producing
trees and shrubs attractive to birds
in autumn and winter, 104; singing
stations, 91; tree- and shrub-nesting,
88; wild bird feeder mix, 108;
winter bird food preferences, 108;
winter bird food recipes, 114-116;

Trees, 70, 88-89, 106, 114, 140-143, 154; hardy trees and shrubs with wildlife values, 135; in planning, 5, 128; trees and shrubs attractive to birds in autumn and winter, 104; trees and shrubs for northern locations, 136
Trembling aspen, 14
Trumpet creeper, 75
Tui Malila, 56
Turtles, 53, 56, 167; box, 55; painted, 55; pond, 55

U

United States Fish and Wildlife Service, 90

V

Vegetables (See Fruits and vegetables attractive to wildlife)
Viceroy, 14, 19
View, avenue of, 124, 126
Violets, 12
Viper's bugloss, 29
Virginia creeper, 135
Virginia opossums, 61
Voles, 63, 155

W

Walnut, 15
Warblers, 168
Wasps, 86; discouraging, 156; eliminating, 78, 158
Water, 4; for balconies and patios, 120; for birdbaths, 95; for butterflies, 9; for hummingbirds, 80; for small mammals, 70; for summer birds, 95; providing for birds in winter, 116; source for pools, 30, 40; sources, 126; sprinklers, 97
Water beetles, 33
Water lilies, 38, 41, 42, 120

Water plantain, 43
Water smartweed, 43
Watershield, 42
Waterweed, Canada, 42
Water-milfoil, 42
Water-parsley, 43
Weeds, 5, 16, 131 132; developing a weed patch, 132
Weigela, 76, 134
White admiral, 13
White tortoiseshell, 12
White, Gilbert, 1
White-footed mice, 63, 155
Whole wheat, 110
Wild celery, 43
Wild cherry, 11
Wild lilac, 16
Wildlife: agency, 144; and disease, 170; needs, 3; orphaned, 161; protection from; 145-147; protection of, 147-159
Wildlife corridors, 125
Wildlife garden, making official, 144
Willows, 11, 13, 14, 15, 19, 29, 43, 134, 137
Wilson's warbler, 6
Winter feeding station, operating, 106
Woodpeckers: 83, 87, 92, 103, 112, 130, 134, 146; damage from, 146; mix, 115
Woolly bear caterpillar, 17
Worms, earth, 137; red wiggler, 138
Wrens, 83, 85, 86, 130, 168

Y

Yarrow, 16
Yellow-jackets, 27
Yew tree, 100, 101

Z

Zoning, 125

About the Author

Born and raised in British Columbia, William J. Merilees first realized his love of wildlife through a membership in the Vancouver Natural History Society. His involvement in scouting and encouragement from his parents, coupled with his own desire to explore nature, bloomed into a lifelong career.

He completed his Bachelors of Science with a special interest in zoology and biology at the University of British Columbia and a Masters of Science at Colorado State University. From teaching at Selkirk Regional College to working as a visitor services officer for BC Parks, Bill was constantly in touch with nature. Now retired, he continues to document and write about the wildlife of Vancouver Island.

Bill's accomplishments include awards for outstanding services from the Federation of BC Naturalists, the Kootenay Doukhobor Historical Society, and the Nanaimo Field Naturalists. His books include *The Humpback Whales of the Georgia Straight* and *Trees, Shrubs and Flowers to Know in British Columbia and Washington*.

When Bill is not in his backyard, he can be found engrossed in a natural history book, studying wildlife or pursuing environmental conservation efforts.